# Coping With Anxiety

## A Practical Guide for Young Adults

Flora F. Manz

information contained within this document, including, but not limited to, errors, omissions, or inaccuracies.

# Table of Contents

# Introduction

## Understanding Anxiety

Imagine waking up every day with a heavy heart and a mind that refuses to quiet down. Picture yourself trying to engage in a simple conversation, only for your thoughts to spiral into endless what-ifs and worst-case scenarios. This is the daily reality for millions of people grappling with anxiety. Whether it's the gnawing feeling of dread when stepping into a crowded place or the overwhelming fear before an important exam, these moments are all too real for those who live with anxiety daily.

Anxiety disorders are among the most common mental health issues affecting individuals today, often remaining hidden behind composed facades and forced smiles. For instance, Lisa's story resonates with many; she battles panic attacks at work while trying to maintain her professional demeanor. These episodes make it difficult for her to navigate through her work responsibilities effectively without feeling overwhelmed. The pressure to perform well and meet the expectations of her job amplifies her anxiety, leading to moments of distress that disrupt her daily routine.

For Lisa, identifying the triggers of her panic attacks is crucial in managing her feelings at work. These triggers could stem from various sources, such as excessive workload, tight deadlines, or interpersonal conflicts with colleagues. By recognizing the cause, she can take proactive steps to address these stressors and alleviate the intensity of her panic attacks.

In *Coping With Anxiety*, we will delve into the multifaceted world of anxiety. We will explore its prevalence and the profound impact it has on various aspects of life. By understanding the gravity, we aim to establish a foundation of trust and authority, offering practical strategies and therapeutic techniques to help manage it effectively. Through relatable stories and evidence-based practices, we will guide you toward reclaiming control and fostering a healthier mindset. Let's embark on this journey together, recognizing that acknowledging and managing anxiety is both necessary and achievable.

## The Pervasiveness of Anxiety

Anxiety disorders affect millions worldwide, yet they often remain invisible, as people tend to suffer in silence. In fact, did you know that in any given year, about 19.1% of U.S. adults experience an anxiety disorder (*Any Anxiety Disorder*, n.d.)? This staggering statistic highlights how common these struggles are, underscoring the importance of addressing mental health issues head-on.

The impact is profound and far-reaching, affecting individuals of all ages and backgrounds. According to Borwin Bandelow, an expert in the field of psychiatry, "Anxiety disorders are the most prevalent mental disorders and are associated with immense health care costs and a high burden of disease" (Bandelow et al., para 39, 2022). When left unmanaged, anxiety can wreak havoc on various aspects of life.

From school-going teens feeling the pressure of academic expectations to professionals juggling demanding careers, anxiety knows no boundaries. For instance, students might find themselves stressing over grades and social acceptance, leading to avoidance behaviors or even refusing to go to school. Adolescents, in particular, are highly affected, with an estimated 31.9% experiencing some form of anxiety disorder (*Anxiety Disorders*, 2022). This can severely impact their educational performance and social interactions, sometimes leading to substance abuse or alcohol use as a coping mechanism.

Adults face their own challenges, balancing work responsibilities, family obligations, and personal well-being. Job stress is a significant contributor, often manifesting as chronic anxiety. Over time, this can impair professional relationships, reduce productivity, and worsen overall mental health. Long-term consequences of untreated anxiety include strained relationships, diminished quality of life, and an increased risk of multiple chronic conditions such as depression and cardiovascular diseases.

Recent studies have shown a worrying trend: Anxiety rates are on the rise. In a survey by the Anxiety and Depression Association of America, it was found that specific phobias affect 9.1% of the U.S. population, and generalized anxiety disorder affects 3.1% (2022). Even more concerning, many individuals delay seeking help for years due to stigma and unawareness about available treatments.

It's crucial to recognize these disorders don't just disappear with age. On the contrary, older adults often face anxiety related to traumatic events, such as a fall or acute illness, with generalized anxiety disorder being particularly common in this demographic (*Anxiety Disorders*, 2022). This not only underscores the persistent nature of anxiety but also highlights the necessity for effective management strategies.

One of the significant reasons for rising anxiety levels is the fast-paced, highly competitive modern lifestyle. Today, individuals are perpetually connected through technology, yet this connectivity often breeds isolation and constant comparison. Social media platforms, while valuable for staying in touch, can amplify feelings of inadequacy, contributing to a societal culture steeped in stress.

To effectively manage anxiety, one must adopt a multifaceted approach. Therapy remains one of the most effective treatments. Cognitive-behavioral therapy (CBT) is particularly beneficial, helping individuals challenge and change unhelpful thought patterns. Medications, such as selective serotonin reuptake inhibitors (SSRIs), can also play a role in alleviating symptoms when prescribed appropriately by a healthcare provider.

Complementary and alternative treatments are also gaining popularity. Practices like mindfulness meditation, yoga, and tai chi can promote relaxation and encourage being present in the moment, which can help break the cycle of anxious thoughts.

Moreover, lifestyle changes can make a significant difference. Regular physical activity, maintaining a balanced diet, and ensuring adequate sleep contribute positively to mental health. Avoiding excessive caffeine and alcohol can also prevent exacerbation of anxiety symptoms.

Support systems are vital also. Engaging with friends, family, or support groups can provide emotional backing and practical advice. Sharing experiences with those who understand fosters a sense of belonging and reduces feelings of isolation. For young adults, connecting with peers facing similar struggles can be particularly empowering.

Lastly, self-awareness and self-compassion are key. Recognizing early signs of anxiety and acknowledging them without judgment can lead to proactive management. It's essential to remind oneself that seeking help is a sign of strength, not weakness.

As we delve deeper into these topics, remember that these tools and techniques have been chosen for their empirical support and practical applicability. Trusting the process and consistently applying these strategies can yield meaningful improvements in managing anxiety.

Your journey doesn't have to be solitary or hopeless. By embracing evidence-based methods and sharing success stories, we aim to provide you with a reliable guide to overcoming anxiety and reclaiming your peace of mind.

You possess the power to transform your experience with anxiety. With patience, persistence, and the right strategies, you can carve out a path toward a healthier, more balanced life. Remember, progress takes time, but every small step forward brings you closer to the calm and control you seek.

# Setting the Stage for Your Journey

It's essential to recognize the importance of addressing these issues head-on. If left unmanaged, anxiety doesn't just affect individual well-being but can ripple out to influence broader societal health. The rising rates of these disorders, exacerbated by our fast-paced modern lifestyle, indicate a pressing concern that warrants attention from both personal and systemic levels.

The consequences of ignoring anxiety are significant. When left untreated, it can lead to strained personal relationships, decreased job performance, and an overall diminished quality of life. On a larger scale, the cumulative effect contributes to increased healthcare costs and a society struggling under the weight of unspoken mental health challenges.

However, there is hope. By embracing evidence-based therapeutic practices, supportive networks, and healthy lifestyle changes, individuals can take concrete steps toward managing their anxiety. Cognitive-behavioral techniques, mindfulness exercises, and the adoption of balanced routines offer practical pathways to reclaiming control and fostering resilience.

Ultimately, your journey with anxiety is deeply personal, yet universally understood. The tools and methods discussed here are designed to empower you, instilling confidence that progress is possible. Remember, seeking help is a sign of strength, and every small step you take brings you closer to a life where anxiety no longer dictates your daily existence.

In closing, consider this: The path to managing anxiety is ongoing, filled with both challenges and triumphs. Embrace self-awareness, seek support, and trust in the process. Your commitment to understanding and addressing your anxiety can pave the way for a healthier, more fulfilling life, helping you not just survive, but truly thrive!

# Chapter 1:

# Understanding Anxiety and

# Its Impact

Have you ever felt your heart race before a big presentation or avoided social gatherings out of sheer dread? These everyday scenarios can often trigger feelings of anxiety that are hard to shake. Although natural at times, these anxious feelings can heavily influence various aspects of our lives, from our thoughts and emotions to our behavior and decision-making processes. Understanding what triggers these moments is the first step toward managing them effectively.

This chapter delves deep into the root causes and manifestations of anxiety in our daily lives. We'll explore how different environmental factors and past traumas contribute to heightened anxiety levels and discuss practical steps to recognize these triggers. From identifying physical signs, like an increased heart rate, to understanding emotional responses, such as fear and worry, we'll cover it all. Additionally, you'll find strategies for developing personalized coping mechanisms, enabling you to manage anxiety sustainably rather than just reacting to it when it strikes. Through this exploration, you'll gain valuable insights into handling your thoughts and emotions, making it easier to navigate life's challenges with confidence and resilience.

# Recognizing Common Triggers

Understanding and addressing anxiety is crucial, especially in our modern world, where stressors seem omnipresent. Picking up on triggers, such as job stress or relationship issues, can significantly help individuals foresee and prepare for potential anxiety-provoking situations. Think of it like being a weather forecaster for your emotions: if you know a storm is likely, you can take shelter before the rains begin.

Here's what you can do to recognize these triggers:

- Start by keeping a journal. Note down moments when you felt anxious and what was happening around you at that time.

- Pay attention to your body's responses. Anxiety often manifests physically, so learn to detect early warning signs such as increased heart rate or sweating.

- Reflect on past experiences. Sometimes, looking back can help you identify patterns. Did certain events or types of interactions consistently trigger anxiety?

- Seek feedback from those close to you. People around you often notice things you might miss.

Understanding how environmental factors or past traumas can influence present anxiety levels lays a solid foundation for personalized coping strategies. Let's face it: Life is full of environmental stressors—everything from the hustle and bustle of city living to significant life changes like moving homes or changing jobs can affect one's mental state.

Past traumas also play a key role in current anxiety levels. Traumatic experiences engrain deep impressions in our psyche, sometimes surfacing years later. Understanding that these past pains influence today's feelings empowers individuals to seek specific therapies that cater to these unique needs.

Identifying triggers enables one to address underlying issues and work toward long-term anxiety management. It's akin to finding the root of a weed and pulling it out entirely rather than repeatedly cutting off the visible parts. When you know what's causing your worry, you can start to address the core problems instead of dealing with symptoms alone.

By acknowledging triggers proactively, individuals can minimize their impact on overall well-being. This means taking steps before anxiety becomes overwhelming, much like maintaining a car to prevent it from breaking down. It's not just about recognizing the triggers but also implementing measures to reduce their influence. It's important to remember that recognizing and understanding triggers is the first step in effectively managing anxiety. Knowing what sets you off gives you the power to prepare, respond, and ultimately reduce its impact on your daily life. This proactive approach transforms you from reacting to anxiety after it hits to managing it sustainably.

Empirical evidence indicates that awareness and preparation are vital in managing anxiety. For instance, a study cited by the National Institute of Mental Health (*Anxiety Disorders*, n.d.) states that people who can anticipate stressful events can mitigate their adverse effects more effectively. Similarly, understanding one's own psychology, including past traumas and environmental influences, offers a personalized roadmap to navigate stressful terrains (Felman, 2023).

Addressing anxiety isn't a linear process; it's more of a journey with peaks and valleys. There will be good days and bad days, but each step you take toward recognizing and understanding your triggers is progress. Empathy toward oneself during this process cannot be overstated. We're all on a journey, and every effort counts.

An evidence-driven approach to managing anxiety allows individuals to contribute more effectively to society in the context of personal freedom and social responsibility. When we manage our anxieties, we're better friends, family members, and colleagues with clearer minds and stronger emotional resilience.

Understanding common triggers, the influence of environmental factors and past traumas, and ways to proactively acknowledge and address these triggers can pave the path toward effective anxiety management. Recognizing and addressing triggers provides a necessary map for navigating life's challenges, ensuring that we can achieve not just economic growth but also prioritize human welfare and well-being. Such balanced strides forward lead to a more harmonious and fulfilling life for everyone involved.

## Understanding Physical and Emotional Effects

When you think about the term "anxiety," what comes to mind? For many, it's an overarching sense of dread or worry. But like most things in life, there's more beneath the surface. It isn't just an emotion; it's a complex interplay of physical and emotional responses. Understanding these dimensions can be the first step toward managing it effectively.

Let's begin with the physiological responses to anxiety. Imagine you're standing at the edge of a high cliff. Your heart races, your muscles tighten, and your breathing quickens. These are all signs that your body is on high alert. It's gearing up for what's often called the "fight-or-flight" response. In our modern lives, however, this response can kick in during non-threatening situations, like speaking up in a meeting or rushing to meet a deadline. Recognizing these early signs can help you intervene before they escalate into more severe symptoms.

Here is what you can do to achieve this:

- Pay attention to your body's signals. Are you noticing a sudden increase in your heart rate? Is there a tightness in your muscles?

- Practice deep-breathing exercises to calm your nervous system.

- Engage in regular physical activity; it helps regulate your body's stress response.

- Create a relaxation routine that includes activities like yoga or meditation.

Acknowledging these physical manifestations is a vital part of keeping anxiety in check. When you become attuned to your body's signals, you can take steps to mitigate them, preventing the situation from spiraling out of control.

But let's not forget about the emotional toll that anxiety takes. Feelings of fear and worry are more than just uncomfortable—they can be downright paralyzing. Internalizing these emotions makes it harder to concentrate, make decisions, or even enjoy daily activities. These feelings don't exist in a vacuum; they're connected to how you think and perceive your world.

Understanding that your emotions have significant weight can empower you to address them head-on. It's okay to feel worried or scared, but acknowledging these feelings rather than suppressing them can make a big difference. Talk about your worries with someone you trust. Sometimes, just verbalizing your fears can lessen their power over you. Cognitive-behavioral techniques can also be helpful. Challenge those irrational thoughts and replace them with more balanced perspectives.

Now, consider the interconnectedness of physical and emotional symptoms. When you're anxious, it isn't just your mind that's affected—your entire body gets involved. This holistic nature of anxiety means that treating just one aspect might not be enough. You need a comprehensive approach that addresses both the mind and the body.

Here is what you can do to address both aspects holistically:

- Combine physical exercises with mindfulness practices. Activities like tai chi or walking meditation can bridge the gap between physical and emotional well-being.

- Ensure you maintain a healthy diet, as nutritional imbalances can exacerbate anxiety symptoms.

- Regularly engage in hobbies that promote both mental and physical wellness. Whether it's a creative activity like painting or a physical one like dancing, find what works best for you.

- Seek professional help when needed. Therapists who specialize in anxiety can offer strategies tailored to both your physical and emotional symptoms.

By learning to identify these manifestations, you can intervene early and prevent escalating symptoms. Think of it as building a toolkit filled with strategies to draw from whenever anxiety rears its head. Notice when it starts to build and employ your go-to techniques: maybe a brisk walk, perhaps a chat with a friend, or even a few minutes of focused breathing.

Recognizing the signs of an anxiety attack as they start gives you the upper hand. Early intervention can transform what could be a full-blown bout of anxiety into a manageable moment. Understanding that it's okay—not just okay, but necessary—to seek support when you feel overwhelmed can bring relief. You're not meant to manage it all by yourself. Reach out to healthcare providers for therapies that suit you best, whether that's counseling, medication, or alternative treatments like acupuncture or biofeedback.

In essence, the awareness of the physical and emotional manifestations of anxiety strengthens your self-monitoring abilities, leading to timely interventions. It's like planting seeds of resilience that will grow stronger with practice and time. Every time you successfully manage an episode, you're reinforcing your ability to handle future ones.

We live in a fast-paced world where stressors are abundant. Knowing how to pinpoint the roots and branches of your anxiety—the physiological tremors, the emotional upheavals—puts you back in the driver's seat of your own life. The more you practice these techniques, the more they become second nature, making it easier to navigate through life's turbulent times with confidence and grace.

By addressing both the physical sensations and the emotional turmoil, we can adopt a more rooted, balanced approach to well-being. Remember, understanding anxiety in a detailed and empathetic manner doesn't eliminate the problem, but it certainly equips you with the tools to manage it better. So, each time you feel anxiety creeping in, reach into your toolkit, apply what you've learned, and remind yourself that you have the power to steer your life in the direction you want.

## The Role of Cognitive Patterns

Let's look at the relationship between thoughts and anxiety, particularly how our cognitive patterns can fuel anxiety. Understanding this connection is essential to grasping how we can manage and reduce stress in our everyday lives.

Negative thought patterns often play a pivotal role in amplifying anxiety. These patterns, known as cognitive distortions, can lead us to view situations through a skewed lens. Common examples include catastrophizing, where we imagine the worst possible outcome, and black-and-white thinking, where we see things in extremes without recognizing the middle ground. Identifying these patterns is the first step toward overcoming them, and you can start by implementing these four steps:

- First, take a moment to notice when you're feeling anxious and try to identify the thought that triggered it.

- Look closely at your thoughts and examine if there's any distortion. Are you blowing things out of proportion (catastrophizing) or seeing things in absolutes (black-and-white thinking)?

- Once you've identified a distortion, challenge it by asking yourself what evidence you have for and against this thought. Is there a more balanced way to look at the situation?

- Lastly, practice reframing your thoughts. For instance, if you're thinking, "I'll never be good at this," shift it to something more constructive like, "I'm still learning, and I can improve with time and practice."

Addressing these negative patterns will help you see shifts in how you think, feel, and react to different situations. Research supports this approach, showing that it's effective in reducing symptoms of depression and anxiety (*Could Negative Thinking Patterns*, n.d.).

## *Thoughts, Emotions, and Behaviors*

Thoughts are powerful as they heavily influence our emotions and behaviors, creating a cycle that uplifts or pulls us down. When you perceive an event negatively, your emotions will likely follow suit, leading to anxious feelings.

This emotional response then influences your behavior—perhaps making you avoid situations that trigger anxiety, which only reinforces your initial negative thoughts.

Take, for example, someone who thinks, "I'll embarrass myself if I speak up in this meeting." This thought causes anxiety, which might lead them to remain silent, reinforcing the belief that they can't handle public speaking. Understanding this cycle highlights the importance of cognitive interventions.

Cognitive-behavioral techniques, such as cognitive restructuring, are vital tools in shifting these maladaptive thought processes. This restructuring involves identifying irrational or harmful thoughts and replacing them with more rational, balanced ones (Curtiss et al., 2021).

The following strategies show you how to engage in cognitive restructuring:

- Start by keeping a thought journal where you note down distressing thoughts as they occur.

- Review these thoughts regularly and write down alternative, more balanced ways to understand the situations.

- Practice these new thoughts consistently so they become more automatic.

- Over time, these balanced thoughts will replace the old, negative ones, making you feel less anxious and more in control.

Employing these strategies consistently can lead to significant improvements in mental well-being. They provide practical steps to challenge negativity and foster a healthier mindset through repetition and reinforcement.

## *Regaining Control Over Thoughts and Emotions*

When individuals tackle their cognitive distortions head-on, they gradually regain control over their thoughts and emotions. This sense of control can substantially lessen anxiety levels, which is both empowering and liberating. It's about understanding that while you can't always control external situations, you can control your reactions and perceptions.

Imagine facing a scenario at work where a project didn't go as planned. Instead of spiraling into thoughts like, "I'm a failure; nothing ever works out for me," reframing can change the narrative. Consider thinking, "This project had challenges, but I learned valuable lessons that will help next time." Such a shift diminishes hopelessness and boosts resilience, making anxieties feel more manageable.

Moreover, studies have shown that cognitive interventions reduce anxiety and improve overall life satisfaction and emotional regulation capabilities (Robinson et al., 2013). When we're equipped to handle stressors realistically and calmly, our interactions and decisions become smoother and more positive.

Changing negative thought patterns has a profound impact on managing anxiety and enhancing overall mental health. Recognizing and challenging cognitive distortions through structured techniques empowers us to break free from the cycle of anxiety. Refocusing our thoughts and perceptions gives us the best chance to foster a more balanced, less anxious state of being.

Taking these steps may not yield instant results, but with consistent practice, the changes can be transformative. Remember, it's okay to seek support along the way. Therapy, especially cognitive-behavioral therapy (CBT), is an excellent resource for those needing guided intervention to tackle deeply ingrained thought patterns.

Ultimately, the goal is to cultivate an environment of empathy and self-compassion while navigating our mental landscapes. Understanding and reworking our cognitive processes is how we build pathways to calmer, more resilient futures.

## Anxiety's Impact on Decision-Making

Anxiety is an intricate part of many young adults' lives, and understanding its root causes and manifestations can be a game-changer in handling daily stressors. One of the significant ways anxiety affects us is through decision-making and behavior, often without our realization. Let's explore how this works and why self-awareness can be pivotal in managing these responses.

When anxiety sets in, our minds can become clouded by cognitive biases. These biases are like mental shortcuts that can lead us to impulsive decisions. For instance, you might overestimate the likelihood of negative outcomes just because you're feeling anxious. This heightened sense of dread can push you toward making hasty choices that provide immediate relief but are not necessarily beneficial in the long run. To counteract these tendencies, mindfulness and self-reflection become vital tools. By taking a moment to pause and breathe before making a decision, you allow yourself the space to assess the situation more rationally.

Here's what you can do to practice mindfulness and self-reflection:

- Take deep breaths and ground yourself in the present moment.

- Acknowledge your feelings without judgment; recognize that it's okay to feel anxious.

- Reflect on past similar situations and the outcomes of your previous decisions.

- Consider writing down your thoughts to organize them better and see patterns you might miss otherwise.

Moreover, anxiety doesn't only play tricks with our thoughts; it can also influence our behavior. Think about times when you've felt an overwhelming urge to avoid certain social situations or lost your temper over minor inconveniences—these are classic examples of anxiety-driven behaviors. Awareness of these tendencies can significantly empower you. Recognizing when you're avoiding something due to anxiety allows you to challenge yourself gently and adopt more adaptive strategies. Instead of dodging that social event, decide to attend, but give yourself permission to leave early if it gets too much. Small steps like these help build resilience over time.

Understanding the relationship between anxiety and your decision-making processes can guide you in developing effective strategies to manage your responses. For example, it might make you overly cautious, preventing you from taking risks that could lead to personal growth. Conversely, it might compel you to take reckless actions to escape the discomfort it brings. Balancing this act requires a thoughtful approach.

Develop strategies to mitigate these behaviors by:

- setting clear, realistic goals for yourself. Break tasks into smaller, manageable chunks.

- using a decision-making matrix to weigh the pros and cons of a choice logically rather than emotionally.

- seeking feedback from trusted friends or mentors who can offer a different perspective.

Another powerful tool in your arsenal is increasing self-awareness about how anxiety influences your behavior. When you understand the triggers and patterns, you gain greater control over your responses. For instance, if you notice a spike during team meetings, preparing notes in advance might help ease your nerves and boost your confidence.

By following these steps, you can cultivate greater control over anxiety-induced behaviors:

- Keep a journal to track your anxiety levels and identify specific triggers.

- Practice relaxation techniques such as progressive muscle relaxation or guided imagery.

- Engage in regular physical activity, which has been proven to reduce symptoms.

- Develop a strong support network of friends, family, or support groups where you can share your experiences and gain insights.

Increased self-awareness provides a clearer picture of how anxiety impacts daily life and decision-making. As you become more attuned to these patterns, making informed choices and fostering adaptive behaviors becomes easier. This might sound initially like a gradual process, but remember, it's a gradual process. The goal isn't to eliminate anxiety but to manage its influence effectively, allowing you to live a fuller, more balanced life.

Empirical research supports these approaches. Studies have shown that individuals who engage in mindfulness experience reduced anxiety and improved decision-making capabilities (Hartley & Phelps, 2012). Similarly, understanding the complex interplay between stress and social decision-making has highlighted the importance of emotional regulation strategies (Wu et al., 2012). For instance, highly socially anxious individuals may benefit from exposure therapy combined with cognitive behavioral techniques to address avoidance behaviors (Hengen & Alpers, 2021).

Ultimately, becoming aware of how anxiety shapes your cognitive and behavioral patterns is empowering. It's an invitation to take proactive steps toward managing your life with greater clarity and intention. So, next time you find yourself overwhelmed, remember these strategies and guidelines. They are your toolkit for navigating these complexities, helping you steer your decisions and behaviors in a direction that serves your long-term well-being.

## Reflecting on Anxiety: Steps Toward Effective Management

Throughout this chapter, we have examined anxiety's root causes and manifestations in our everyday lives. We've laid a foundation for effectively managing it by recognizing common triggers and understanding how past traumas and environmental factors shape our responses.

However, it's essential to acknowledge that this journey isn't straightforward. Some readers might be concerned about the overwhelming tasks of self-awareness and implementing coping mechanisms. It's perfectly normal to feel daunted by these steps but remember, every effort counts. Progress is not linear; there will be peaks and valleys, moments of breakthrough, and times when it feels like two steps back.

On a broader scale, effectively managing our anxiety doesn't only impact our personal well-being—it enhances our social interactions and contributions to our communities. By fostering a balanced mind, we're able to approach life's challenges with grace and resilience, making us better friends, partners, and colleagues.

As we conclude this chapter, let's embrace the idea that understanding our anxiety provides us the map we need to steer through life's complexities. While the path may be winding and occasionally steep, each mindful step brings us closer to a harmonious and fulfilling life. Remember, you have the power to navigate your emotional landscape, shaping your destiny one thoughtful decision at a time. So, keep that toolkit handy, and don't hesitate to seek support along the way. Your journey toward peace and balance is an ongoing adventure filled with learning and growth.

In the next chapter, we will explore evidence-based therapies and tools for managing anxiety on a daily basis.

# Chapter 2:

# Practical Tools for Managing

# Anxiety

Anxiety often manifests as persistent worry, fear, or unease. Various situations, whether it's an upcoming exam, social interactions, or personal challenges, can trigger these feelings. For example, imagine you're preparing for a big presentation at work. Your mind fixates on negative outcomes: "What if I forget my lines?" or "Everyone will think I'm incompetent." These thoughts can spiral out of control, creating a self-fulfilling prophecy and making it hard to perform at your best. Recognizing and addressing these patterns is crucial because unchecked anxiety can lead to significant stress and decreased quality of life.

In this chapter, you'll discover actionable steps to challenge these negative thought patterns and replace them with more realistic and balanced ones. Additionally, you'll learn relaxation exercises and visualization techniques, like deep breathing and progressive muscle relaxation, to help calm your body and mind during stressful times. By integrating these practices into your daily routine, you can build emotional resilience and a more balanced perspective, empowering you to navigate life's challenges with greater ease.

# Learning Cognitive Restructuring to Challenge Negative Thought Patterns

Cognitive restructuring involves identifying negative thought patterns and replacing them with more balanced and realistic thoughts through evidence-based techniques. This might sound a bit technical, but it's rooted in simple, actionable steps you can take daily, such as:

- Begin by spotting the negative thoughts that cause distress. These could be about yourself, others, or situations.

- Next, question these thoughts. Are they based on fact or assumption? Asking yourself if there's concrete evidence supporting these thoughts can be illuminating.

- Then, replace these negative thoughts with more realistic ones. Instead of thinking, "I will fail this exam," try, "I have prepared well for this exam, and I will do my best."

This process doesn't need to be overwhelming. Start small, perhaps by keeping a journal where you jot down distressing thoughts and work through these steps. Over time, this practice can become a natural part of your thinking process.

Individuals can reduce anxiety and improve their overall mental well-being by challenging distorted thinking. When we allow our minds to be dominated by unexamined negative thoughts, we are essentially giving those thoughts power over us. But when we start questioning these thoughts, we create space for more balanced perspectives to emerge.

Imagine you're constantly worried about public speaking. Your mind might tell you, "Everyone will think I'm an idiot." But what if you challenge that notion? Ask yourself: "Is everyone going to really think that?" Some won't pay close attention, while others may relate to your nervousness and appreciate your effort. Taking this slow will help you ease a lot of unnecessary stress.

Practicing cognitive restructuring regularly can lead to a positive shift in mindset and emotional resilience. Instead of automatically jumping to worst-case scenarios, you develop a habit of evaluating situations more objectively. This gradual shift can foster a sense of stability and calmness.

Just like any other skill, this requires practice. It's like going to the gym for your mind.

This might mean setting aside a few minutes each day to reflect on your thoughts. You don't need to write a novel— just note a few instances where you felt anxious or stressed and apply the steps we've discussed. This small effort can significantly impact your overall mental health.

Engaging in cognitive restructuring empowers individuals to take control of their thoughts and emotions. Often, we feel at the mercy of our thoughts, as though they come out of nowhere and dictate our feelings. Cognitive restructuring is a way to regain control.

When you actively decide to challenge and change faulty beliefs, you're taking a stand against automatic negative thinking. This doesn't mean you'll never have another negative thought, but it does mean you'll be better equipped to handle them when they do arise.

Imagine that you are working through social anxiety. You might begin with very mild exposure, perhaps just saying "hello" to a colleague. Over weeks, using cognitive restructuring, you might learn to question your negative thoughts associated with these interactions. Gradually, this practice builds your confidence and reduces the hold anxiety has over them.

This technique helps develop emotional resilience too. Life will always throw curveballs, but with cognitive restructuring, you build a toolkit that helps you navigate these challenges more effectively.

Remember that cognitive restructuring isn't about ignoring negative thoughts. Rather, it's about ensuring our thinking aligns more closely with reality, enriching our lives with balanced and constructive perspectives. Taking the initiative to regularly practice these steps paves the way for lasting emotional health.

## Practicing Relaxation Exercises and Visualization for Stress Reduction

Relaxation exercises such as deep breathing and progressive muscle relaxation can help calm the mind and body during times of stress. When we're overwhelmed, our bodies react with a "fight or flight" response, making it challenging to stay composed. These techniques offer practical tools to counter this reaction.

Deep breathing is straightforward yet immensely effective. It involves taking slow, deliberate breaths to increase oxygen flow and promote a state of calm. To begin, find a comfortable position—sitting or lying down. Close your eyes if it helps. Inhale deeply through your nose, allowing your abdomen to expand fully. Hold your breath for a moment, then slowly exhale through your mouth. Imagine you're blowing away the stress with each exhalation. Repeat this cycle several times until you feel more relaxed.

Progressive muscle relaxation requires a similar foundational calm but adds an element of intentional tension and release in specific muscle groups. Start by tensing the muscles in your toes, holding the tension for about five seconds, then releasing it slowly while focusing on the sensation of relaxation. Move methodically up your body—feet, legs, stomach, arms, and face. By the time you reach your head, the cumulative effect is a deeply relaxed state. It's like teaching your body the difference between tension and relaxation, enabling you to recognize and reduce stress better.

Visualization techniques involve imagining peaceful scenes or positive outcomes to promote feelings of relaxation and well-being. The idea is to use the power of your mind to transport yourself to a place of serenity. Visualization can be particularly effective because our brains often can't distinguish between what we vividly imagine and what's real.

Here is a short visualization exercise that you can do right now. Begin this practice by finding a quiet spot where you won't be disturbed. Close your eyes and take a few deep breaths to center yourself. Then, picture a scene that feels calming to you—it could be a beach, a forest clearing, or even a cozy room. Engage all your senses to make this mental escape vivid. Hear the waves crashing or birds chirping, feel the warmth of the sun or the softness of a blanket, smell the ocean breeze or the scent of pine trees. The more detailed and immersive your visualization, the more effective it will be. Take a deep breath and open your eyes. Notice how you are feeling.

Visualization can also involve imagining successful outcomes in situations that usually cause anxiety. Perhaps you have an upcoming presentation that's stressing you out. Visualize yourself delivering your speech confidently, seeing the audience nodding in agreement, and feeling a sense of accomplishment afterward. This calms you in the moment and builds your confidence for the actual event.

Regular practice of relaxation and visualization techniques can reduce physiological arousal and enhance overall emotional stability. It's important to note that these techniques are skills—you get better at them with practice. Just like learning a musical instrument or a new language, consistency is key.

Start by setting aside a few minutes each day to practice. You don't need a lot of time; even five to ten minutes can make a difference. Over time, you'll likely find that you can calm yourself more quickly and easily. There might be days when your mind wanders or you find it hard to relax—that's okay. What's important is showing up for yourself consistently.

Incorporating these techniques into daily routines can serve as an effective coping mechanism for managing anxiety. Life's demands won't disappear, but your ability to handle them can improve dramatically. Perhaps you start your morning with a few minutes of deep breathing or end your day with a session of progressive muscle relaxation. You can also weave them into moments throughout the day.

The beauty of these tools is their flexibility—they can be done almost anywhere, anytime, without any special equipment. They empower you to take control of your mental well-being actively. And while they're simple, their impact can be profound, fostering resilience and emotional balance.

Research supports the efficacy of these techniques. According to the Mayo Clinic, relaxation techniques can lower heart rate, reduce blood pressure, and decrease stress hormone levels (Mayo Clinic Staff, 2024). Moreover, studies show that methods like progressive muscle relaxation and deep breathing significantly reduce anxiety and improve psychological states (Toussaint et al., 2021). To benefit most from these methods:

- create a consistent routine. Find a time each day when you can dedicate a few minutes to practice.

- be patient with yourself. It's normal for your mind to wander. Gently bring your focus back to your breath or visualization.

- adapt the techniques to what works best for you. Maybe you prefer visualizing a mountain lake instead of a beach or find comfort in guided audio recordings.

- keep practicing even if you don't see immediate results. Like any skill, it takes time to build proficiency and experience long-lasting benefits.

By embedding these practices into your daily life, you're not just managing stress in the moment. You're cultivating a healthier relationship with your mind and emotions, providing a sturdy foundation for navigating life's challenges with greater ease and resilience.

## Utilizing Mindfulness Techniques to Increase Awareness and Reduce Anxiety

Mindfulness, at its core, involves staying present in the moment without judgment. Imagine being able to observe your thoughts and emotions like a neutral bystander. Instead of letting these things overwhelm you, you simply notice them. This practice might seem simple, but it can be incredibly powerful.

Here are five basic steps to familiarize yourself with mindfulness:

- Begin by finding a quiet and comfortable place where you won't be disturbed.

- Close your eyes and take a few deep breaths, feeling the air fill up your lungs and then gently leave your body.

- Notice what thoughts come into your mind. Perhaps they're about your day, or maybe they're worries or concerns. Acknowledge these thoughts without trying to change them or push them away.

- When you catch yourself judging your thoughts ("I shouldn't be thinking this" or "Why can't I stop worrying?"), gently bring your attention back to your breath and remind yourself that it's okay to have these thoughts.

- Continue observing without engaging. If an emotion arises, note how it feels in your body. For instance, anxiety might feel like a tightness in your chest or a pit in your stomach. Simply acknowledge it and let it be.

This simple technique helps you notice your thoughts and feelings without getting caught up in them. This awareness can reduce the intensity of your emotions over time, allowing you to navigate your inner world with more ease and less stress.

## *Developing Calm through Focused Breathing and Body Scans*

Specific mindfulness practices, such as focused breathing and body scans, can help create a sense of calm and centeredness. These techniques are like mental training exercises that enhance your ability to manage anxiety.

Here's how you can start:

- To practice focused breathing, sit comfortably and place one hand on your chest and the other on your belly. Breathe in slowly through your nose, allowing your belly to rise naturally. Feel the movement of your hands as you inhale and exhale.

- If you find your mind wandering, gently guide it back to your breath. Don't worry if you have to do this multiple times—it's all part of the process.

- For a body scan, lie down in a comfortable position. Close your eyes and take a few deep breaths to settle in. Start by focusing on your toes. Notice any sensations there, whether it's warmth, coolness, tension, or relaxation.

- Gradually move your attention up through your feet, legs, abdomen, chest, arms, and head. Take your time with each body part, acknowledging whatever you sense without judgment. If you encounter areas of tension, breathe into them and imagine releasing the tightness with each exhale.

Engaging in these practices regularly can forge a habit of returning to a state of calm even amidst anxiety. They serve as anchor points that ground you in the present, reducing the overall impact of anxious thoughts and feelings.

### *Daily Mindfulness Practices for Enhanced Self-Awareness*

Incorporating mindfulness into your daily routine doesn't need to be complicated. It's about scheduling intentional pauses, which can lead to greater self-awareness and emotional regulation.

Consider these steps:

- Start your day with a mindful morning routine. As you brush your teeth or make your bed, focus intently on each action. Notice the textures, smells, and sounds involved.

- During meals, eat mindfully. Pay attention to the colors, textures, and flavors of your food. This not only aids digestion but also cultivates a deeper connection to your eating habits.

- Set reminders on your phone to take short mindfulness breaks. These can be as brief as a minute or two. Use this time to check in with your breath, notice any tension in your body, and refocus your mind.

- Before bedtime, reflect on your day. Think about three things you're grateful for and visualize them vividly. This practice promotes positive thinking and helps you wind down for a restful night's sleep.

Consistency is key here. The more frequently you incorporate mindfulness into your routines, the more natural it will become, and the better equipped you'll be to handle anxiety when it arises.

## Acceptance of Internal Experiences

Finally, mindfulness teaches us the importance of accepting our internal experiences. Often, we react to anxiety triggers with resistance or avoidance, which only amplifies our distress. Mindfulness offers a different approach—one of acceptance.

When you accept your internal experiences, you're fostering a non-reactive and compassionate attitude toward anxiety. Here's how you can nurture this mindset:

- When you feel anxiety bubbling up, instead of pushing it away, try saying to yourself, "It's okay to feel this way. I'm human, and it's natural to have these emotions."

- Visualize your anxiety as a wave in the ocean. You don't try to stop the wave; you ride it out. Know that just like waves, your emotions rise and fall.

- Practice self-compassion. Treat yourself as you would treat a dear friend who is going through a tough time. Speak kindly to yourself and acknowledge your efforts in managing anxiety.

- Use affirmations to reinforce acceptance. Simple phrases like "I am doing my best" or "This too shall pass" can be powerful tools in reducing reactivity to anxiety.

Through acceptance, you create space for your feelings without letting them control you. This shift from reaction to acceptance can be profoundly liberating.

The journey of incorporating mindfulness into your life may not always be smooth, but it is undoubtedly rewarding. By using mindfulness techniques, you enhance your self-awareness and promote a sense of inner peace. Remember, it's not about eliminating anxiety completely but developing a healthier relationship with it. Embrace these practices with patience and kindness toward yourself, and gradually, you'll discover a newfound resilience in navigating life's ups and downs.

## Implementing Grounding Techniques During Anxiety-Provoking Situations

Grounding techniques are essential tools for anyone looking to stay anchored in the present moment, particularly during heightened episodes of anxiety.

They involve using sensory cues like focusing on breathing, touch, or surroundings to anchor oneself in the present moment during heightened anxiety. Imagine you're feeling overwhelmed, perhaps a knot of worry has just settled in your stomach. A simple yet effective way to combat this is by paying close attention to your breath.

Close your eyes, if it feels comfortable, and take a slow, deep breath in, counting to four as you do. Hold it for a second, then breathe out just as slowly. Feel the air as it moves through your nostrils, fills your lungs, and finally leaves your body—an immediate, tangible way to ground yourself in the here and now. Another technique might include focusing on physical objects around you. Try touching different textures—perhaps the cool surface of your desk or the softness of a cushion, letting these sensations remind you that you're safe and present.

These grounding exercises can significantly help individuals disengage from overwhelming thoughts and emotions, providing a sense of stability and control. When anxiety hits, our minds tend to spiral, often focusing on uncertainties and worst-case scenarios. By redirecting our attention to something tangible, we can interrupt that spiral.

Think about the 5-4-3-2-1 method—a favorite among many. Start by naming five things you can see around you. Then, four things you can touch. Follow this with three things you can hear. Next, identify two things you can smell. Finally, focus on one thing you can taste. Each step of this exercise gently shifts your attention away from racing thoughts and back to the reality of the present moment (*Grounding Techniques*, n.d.).

Grounding techniques enhance emotional regulation and reduce the intensity of anxiety symptoms in challenging situations. Regular use of these methods can build resilience, offering you a toolbox of strategies to manage stress better. It's not just about handling that single moment of anxiety; it's about creating a habit of grounding that empowers you to face whatever challenges come your way. You could incorporate practices like progressive muscle relaxation, where you systematically tense and then relax each muscle group in your body. This helps you become more aware of physical sensations and can interrupt the feedback loop of stress and tension.

Integrating grounding strategies into everyday life can serve as a vital tool in managing anxiety and promoting a sense of security. Imagine incorporating brief grounding moments into your daily routine. Over time, these small practices can add up, building a foundation of calm and presence that supports you through tougher times.

One practical method for implementing grounding techniques is the hand-on-heart approach. Before starting, find a comfortable position and place your hand gently over your heart. Focus on the warmth of your hand and the steady rhythm of your heartbeat. This simple act can instantly connect you with your physical self and provide a soothing reassurance that you're right here, right now, and okay.

As you continue to integrate these grounding techniques, it's crucial to remember that consistency is key. The more often you practice, the more automatic these responses will become. They will transform from conscious efforts to instinctual habits, ready to support you whenever needed. Remember, there's no one-size-fits-all when it comes to grounding exercises. Some may find deep breathing especially useful, while others might prefer tactile engagement or the structured method of the 5-4-3-2-1 technique. It's all about discovering what resonates most with you and making it a part of your routine.

While grounding techniques are powerful tools, they work best when combined with an overall commitment to self-care and mental health. Ensure you're also getting enough sleep, eating well, staying hydrated, and moving your body regularly. These foundational elements of wellness complement grounding practices and enhance your ability to manage anxiety effectively.

It's also beneficial to have a personalized grounding toolkit. Think of it as a collection of go-to strategies that you can turn to whenever anxiety strikes. Your kit might include a favorite breathing exercise, a calming playlist, a piece of fabric with a soothing texture, or even a list of grounding exercises written down for quick reference. Having these resources readily available can provide a comforting sense of preparedness and control.

Feel free to experiment with different grounding exercises and observe how each one makes you feel. Journaling your experiences can be incredibly insightful. Write about what works for you, what doesn't, and how each technique affects your anxiety levels. Over time, you'll develop a deeper understanding of your unique needs and preferences, fine-tuning your approach to anxiety management.

## Empowering Yourself With Effective Anxiety Management Tools

We've covered the mechanics of cognitive restructuring, which involves identifying negative thought patterns and challenging them with more realistic perspectives. This skill, akin to mental exercise, trains your brain to shift from destructive thinking to balanced outlooks, ultimately helping you regain control over your thoughts and emotions.

We also looked at relaxation exercises, such as deep breathing and progressive muscle relaxation, along with the transformative potential of visualization techniques. Picture calming scenes or visualize positive outcomes to alleviate stress; these approaches can significantly enhance your mental well-being. Regular practice, even for a few minutes each day, turns these exercises into powerful allies against anxiety.

Mindfulness was another significant focus. Staying present in the moment and observing your thoughts without judgment can foster greater self-awareness and reduce the grip of anxious feelings. Techniques like focused breathing and body scans were highlighted as methods to develop calm and maintain emotional balance.

Grounding techniques rounded out our discussion. Using sensory inputs to anchor yourself in the present moment, especially during intense anxiety episodes, gives you a practical way to disengage from overwhelming thoughts. The 5-4-3-2-1 technique and tactile engagement, among others, offer relief by shifting your focus back to the here and now.

What may concern some is the time it takes to see significant improvements. Patience and persistence are crucial—think of these practices as a long-term investment in your mental health. On a broader scale, mastering these techniques can lead to a more balanced and enriched life, positively impacting not just your well-being but also your relationships and productivity.

As you move forward, embrace these strategies with kindness toward yourself. Remember, every small step you take is progress. Your journey toward managing anxiety is unique, and with these tools at your disposal, you're better equipped to face whatever comes your way. What changes might you start noticing if you commit to these practices today? The possibilities are vast and promising.

In the next chapter, we will discuss the importance of emotional resilience when managing anxiety in the long term.

Chapter 3:

# Enhancing Emotional

# Resilience

Imagine standing at the edge of a vast ocean, waves crashing with relentless force. The sea represents the challenges and anxieties we all face, and our ability to float or sink depends on our inner strength. It is in these moments, when the storms of anxiety batter us, that emotional resilience can act as our lifeboat. Cultivating this resilience isn't about avoiding the storm but learning how to navigate it with grace and fortitude.

Anxiety triggers are like sudden squalls—unexpected and overwhelming. They can leave us feeling helpless, caught in a riptide of emotions such as fear, self-doubt, and panic. For instance, a college student might feel paralyzed by the pressure of exams, constantly questioning their capabilities. Or consider a young professional struggling to meet work deadlines, feeling suffocated by the weight of internal and external. These scenarios are just glimpses into the myriad ways anxiety can manifest, leaving individuals feeling drained and powerless. Without effective strategies to cope, these triggers can escalate, making everyday tasks appear insurmountable.

In this chapter, we take a look at practical approaches to bolster emotional resilience and adaptability amid anxiety triggers. We will explore the significance of cultivating self-compassion and acceptance, offering concrete steps to treat oneself with understanding and kindness during anxious times. Additionally, we'll discuss building a supportive network and seeking professional help, invaluable resources for anyone looking to strengthen their emotional foundation.

Finally, we will introduce engaging activities that promote emotional well-being, helping you create a personalized toolkit to manage stress effectively. By the end of this chapter, you'll be equipped with actionable strategies and a renewed perspective on handling anxiety, fostering a resilient mindset ready to face life's inevitable storms.

# Cultivating Self-Compassion and Acceptance

When managing anxiety, one of the most impactful strategies is practicing self-compassion. This might sound like a vague concept at first, but let's break it down.

Self-compassion involves treating yourself with kindness and understanding during moments of anxiety. Imagine how you would speak to a close friend who's having a tough time—now try speaking to yourself that way. For instance:

- When you notice self-critical thoughts creeping in, challenge them with compassionate responses. If you find yourself thinking, "Why am I always so anxious?

What's wrong with me?" counter it with, "I'm doing my best, and it's okay to feel anxious sometimes."

- Actively remind yourself of your strengths and positive attributes. Keep a list of things you've done well to refer to on challenging days.

- Give yourself permission to make mistakes. Everyone errs; it's part of being human. Reframe mistakes as opportunities for growth rather than failures.

While practicing self-compassion can lower levels of anxiety, acceptance of these emotions also plays a crucial role. Acceptance doesn't mean giving up or conceding defeat; it's about acknowledging your feelings without judgment. When an anxiety wave hits, rather than fighting it or labeling it as "bad," try these steps:

- Notice and name your emotions. Simply saying, "I feel anxious," can take some power away.

- Allow yourself to experience these feelings without rushing to change them. Think of them as clouds passing by—you don't need to latch onto them.

- Utilize mindful breathing techniques to ground yourself in the present moment. Focusing on your breath can create a pocket of calm amidst the storm.

Embracing both self-compassion and acceptance establishes a solid foundation for self-care and emotional well-being. When you treat yourself with do this, you're more equipped to handle anxiety with grace and strength. Moreover, by applying these principles consistently, you cultivate an inner resilience that acts as a buffer against future episodes of anxiety.

The importance of cultivating self-compassion in dealing with anxiety cannot be overstated. Studies have shown that individuals who practice self-compassion report lower levels of anxiety and depression (*Self-Acceptance and Self-Compassion*, n.d.). This approach encourages viewing oneself through a lens of empathy and understanding, ultimately leading to better mental health outcomes.

Similarly, fostering acceptance of anxiety by acknowledging and allowing your difficult emotions can be profoundly liberating. It promotes psychological flexibility—one of the key components of emotional resilience (Klein et. al, 2023). To internalize this approach, consider these practical tips:

- Develop an inner dialogue that supports rather than criticizes: Next time you hit a rough patch, ask yourself how you would comfort a friend in the same situation and apply those words to yourself.

- Practice gentle self-talk: Replace thoughts like "I'm failing" with "I'm learning." Present challenges as growth opportunities rather than setbacks.

- Engage in regular self-reflection: Spend uninterrupted time journaling or meditating to become honest with yourself about your feelings and experiences.

True emotional resilience emerges from recognizing our inherent worthiness—accepting ourselves fully, warts and all. It's about moving past the paralyzing grip of self-criticism and embracing a kinder, more forgiving perspective. This shift doesn't just happen overnight, but with persistence and patience, it can transform your relationship with anxiety.

Cultivating self-compassion and acceptance in times of anxiety not only aids in navigating anxiety triggers but also builds a deeper sense of self-worth and emotional stability. By treating yourself with kindness and welcoming your emotions without judgment, you'll discover a path to a more balanced, resilient, and fulfilling life.

Remember, every small step counts. Be patient with yourself, celebrate your progress, and keep moving forward. You're laying the groundwork for lasting emotional health and well-being through self-compassion and acceptance.

# Building a Supportive Network and Seeking Professional Help

Establishing a support system of trusted individuals can offer emotional support and practical assistance during times of heightened anxiety. When we talk about building a support system, it's not just about having people around you; it's about having the right people—those you trust and who understand or are willing to understand what you're going through. It can be incredibly comforting to know that there's someone you can turn to for a listening ear or a shoulder to cry on. This network can include friends, family members, colleagues, or even community members like neighbors or group members in clubs.

A supportive network can be built or maintained through the following strategies:

- Consider starting with those closest to you, such as family and long-time friends. Open up conversations about your experiences with anxiety, and let them know how they can best support you.

- Look into joining local or online groups where you can meet others facing similar challenges. Shared experiences can be a great foundation for mutual support.

- Don't hesitate to reach out to acquaintances and turn them into trusted friends. Sometimes, people whom you might not expect can become significant pillars of support.

- Make an effort to maintain regular contact with these individuals. Regular meetups, calls, or even simple messages can keep your support system robust and engaged.

Seeking professional help from therapists or counselors can provide specialized support and guidance in developing coping strategies for managing anxiety triggers. While having a personal network is invaluable, there are times when professional intervention is necessary.

Mental health professionals have the training and experience to offer evidence-based treatments and techniques tailored to your specific needs. Therapy provides a safe space to explore underlying issues and work on strategies to manage anxiety effectively.

Here are steps you can take to seek professional help:

- Start by researching therapists or counseling services in your area. Many clinics, like the US-based Highland Springs Clinic in Salt Lake Valley and Idaho, offer various programs and treatments, making it easier to find the right fit for your needs (Hood, 2020).

- Don't overlook the importance of finding a therapist with whom you feel comfortable. A good therapeutic relationship is crucial for effective therapy.

- Check whether the service providers accept your insurance or if you qualify for any financial assistance programs, as this can alleviate some affordability-related stress.

- When you find a suitable therapist, schedule an initial consultation to discuss your concerns and treatment goals. This first step can often bring a sense of relief and direction.

Regularly communicating with trusted individuals about anxiety experiences can foster understanding and empathy, strengthening relationships and emotional resilience. Sharing your experiences isn't just about unloading your burdens; it's also about giving those you care about an opportunity to understand what you're dealing with. Honest communication helps dispel misconceptions and build stronger, more empathetic relationships.

Building a strong support network and seeking professional help when needed can significantly enhance emotional resilience and provide valuable resources for managing anxiety triggers effectively.

You don't have to go through this alone. Combining personal support systems and professional guidance creates a holistic approach to mental health care.

Anxiety can make life feel overwhelming, but remember, reaching out to others and accepting help is a sign of strength, not weakness. Building a support network takes time, effort, and sometimes stepping outside your comfort zone. But the benefits—improved well-being, better coping skills, and stronger relationships—are well worth it. With a dedicated support system and professional guidance, you can navigate anxiety more effectively and lead a fulfilling, balanced life.

# Engaging in Activities That Promote Emotional Well-Being

Participating in activities such as physical exercise, mindfulness practices, and hobbies can significantly reduce stress levels and foster a profound sense of well-being. Engaging in these activities might seem simple, but the effects on one's emotional state are profound and scientifically grounded.

For instance, physical exercise releases endorphins, often dubbed the body's natural painkillers and mood elevators. Studies have shown that even short durations of exercise—such as brisk walking or cycling—can trigger this beneficial release.

To get started:

- Begin by setting small, achievable goals for yourself. It could be as simple as taking a 20-minute walk around your neighborhood.

- Incorporate mindfulness practices like meditation or deep-breathing exercises into your daily routine. Apps like Headspace or Calm can guide you through the process if you're new to it.

- Dive into hobbies that spark joy and creativity—whether it's painting, writing, gardening, or playing a musical instrument. These activities serve as excellent diversions from stressors and help maintain a prolonged focus and relaxation.

Prioritizing self-care is equally critical for emotional balance and building resilience against anxiety triggers. To truly thrive emotionally, one must not overlook foundational aspects like sleep, nutrition, and relaxation. The interplay between these elements can determine how well one navigates stress. A solid night's sleep, for example, allows the brain and body to repair, improves cognitive function, and regulates mood. On the other hand, poor nutrition can lead to blood sugar imbalances and inflammatory responses that exacerbate feelings of anxiety and depression.

Here's how you can prioritize self-care:

- Ensure you're getting adequate sleep by sticking to a consistent bedtime routine. Limit screen time before bed and create a calming sleep environment.

- Focus on consuming a balanced diet rich in fruits, vegetables, lean proteins, and whole grains. Avoid excessive caffeine and sugar, which can induce anxiety spikes.

- Incorporate relaxation techniques like taking warm baths, practicing yoga, or listening to soothing music. These activities can lower cortisol levels—the hormone responsible for stress.

While focusing on building emotional resilience, it's also beneficial to incorporate enjoyable and fulfilling activities in your routine. When you engage in tasks that you genuinely enjoy, it distracts you from anxious thoughts and elevates your mood. This diversion is not merely an escape but a deliberate strategy to infuse positivity into your life. Think about what activities make you smile—perhaps spending time with loved ones, reading a captivating book, or exploring nature.

The concept here is not about ignoring our stressors but creating moments that uplift our spirits and provide a mental reprieve. Immersing yourself in fulfilling endeavors can reshape your emotional landscape, leading to a more positive and resilient mindset.

Lastly, incorporating stress-reducing activities into daily routines is essential to develop a personalized toolbox for managing anxiety triggers. Once you identify what works best for you, it's crucial to weave these activities seamlessly into your everyday life. This way should stress arise, you have dependable coping mechanisms readily at hand.

Research supports the efficacy of such techniques. For instance, a study on stress management skills training with college students revealed that regular engagement in structured stress management practices significantly improved their academic vitality and psychological well-being (Abed et al., 2015). Similarly, evidence also highlights that when individuals perceive higher stress levels, engaging in self-care becomes challenging but remains crucial for maintaining well-being (Bermejo-Martins et al., 2021).

Indeed, tackling stress and boosting emotional resilience is less about eliminating all sources of stress and more about enhancing our response to these stressors through manageable, consistent actions. With patience and persistence, these strategies can transform reactive responses into proactive coping mechanisms.

Keeping these concepts and guidelines in mind will empower young adults to effectively manage their emotions, adapt to stressors, and maintain a steady course toward emotional well-being.

As we adopt these evidence-based approaches, we put ourselves in a better position to navigate life's inevitable ups and downs with grace and resilience.

# Exploring the Growth Mindset Concept

When you're grappling with anxiety triggers, it's easy to view challenges as overwhelming obstacles. However, adopting a growth mindset can transform these hurdles into valuable opportunities for learning and growth. Viewing challenges this way doesn't come naturally to everyone, but it is an approach that you can cultivate over time.

Here's what you can do to start:

- Begin by acknowledging the challenge instead of avoiding it. Recognize that every obstacle offers a unique lesson.

- Reframe your thoughts. Instead of thinking, "I can't handle this," try, "What can I learn from this?"

- Seek out resources or people who have successfully navigated similar challenges. Books, online communities, or mentors can be invaluable sources of wisdom and encouragement.

- Practice self-compassion. Understand that struggling with a challenge doesn't make you weak; it makes you human. Give yourself permission to stumble and rise again.

Fostering a growth mindset can help you become more resilient and adaptable when anxiety triggers strike. When you see difficulties as temporary and surmountable, you open yourself up to the possibility of growth, which fosters emotional resilience. Embracing setbacks as learning experiences can also lead to increased self-awareness, personal development, and emotional strength. Setbacks are often viewed negatively, but they provide us with crucial insights into our behaviors, patterns, and areas for improvement.

To embrace setbacks effectively:

- Reflect on each setback. Ask yourself questions like, "What went wrong?" and "What could I have done differently?"

- Consider keeping a journal to document your thoughts and lessons learned. Writing things down can offer clarity and new perspectives.

- Use setbacks as a mirror to understand your strengths and weaknesses better. This self-awareness will guide your future actions and decisions.

- Celebrate small victories along the way. Recognition of even minor progress will keep you motivated and focused on continuous improvement.

By seeing setbacks as valuable learning experiences, you'll begin to appreciate their role in your personal growth. This shift in perspective not only strengthens your emotional foundation but also enhances your capacity to deal with future anxieties constructively.

When facing anxiety, focusing on limitations can feel stifling and discouraging. Adopting a growth mindset allows you to shift your focus from limitations to possibilities, which encourages positive change and constructive problem-solving. Instead of being paralyzed by what you cannot do, you begin to explore what you can achieve.

This shift in perspective helps you realize that limitations are not fixed barriers but hurdles that can be overcome with the right approach and mindset. Constructive problem-solving becomes second nature when you routinely practice seeing beyond your perceived constraints.

Developing a belief in your capacity for growth and development can empower you to face anxiety triggers with optimism and perseverance. When you truly believe that you can improve and adapt, you're more likely to approach challenges with a positive attitude and a willingness to persist despite difficulties.

Empowering yourself starts with cultivating a belief in your growth potential. This approach invites optimism and fortitude, essential elements for navigating through anxiety triggers successfully.

Cultivating resilience and adaptability in the face of anxiety triggers becomes far more achievable when we view our struggles as stepping stones rather than stumbling blocks. By fostering self-awareness, encouraging creative problem-solving, and nurturing a belief in our inherent ability to grow, we chart a pathway to managing anxiety and thriving amidst it.

As you continue on this journey, remember that it's not about avoiding anxiety triggers altogether. Instead, it's about developing the tools and mindset to manage them effectively and emerge stronger from the experience.

# Harnessing Emotional Resilience for Lifelong Well-Being

Throughout this chapter, we've delved into invaluable strategies for building emotional resilience and adaptability in the face of anxiety triggers. We started by exploring the profound impact of cultivating self-compassion and acceptance. By treating ourselves with kindness and understanding, we create a safe internal space that allows us to acknowledge our emotions without judgment. This foundational step is crucial in managing anxiety more effectively.

We've also emphasized the importance of building a supportive network and seeking professional help when needed. Surrounding ourselves with trusted individuals who understand our struggles can provide much-needed emotional support. Additionally, professional guidance from therapists can offer tailored coping strategies that address specific needs, making it easier to navigate through periods of heightened anxiety.

Engaging in activities that promote emotional well-being has been another key focus. Physical exercise, mindfulness practices, and hobbies significantly reduce stress levels and enhance overall mental health. These activities serve as practical tools to ensure that you can maintain emotional balance even amid life's challenges.

As you move forward, remember that each small step counts. Be gentle with yourself, celebrate your progress, and strive for greater emotional well-being. Through consistent practice and a compassionate approach, you're laying a strong foundation for lasting mental health and resilience.

In the next chapter, we will look at effective ways to manage relationships when you are feeling anxious.

# Chapter 4:

# Navigating Relationships During Anxiety

Imagine you're sitting at a café, the hum of conversations around you mingling with the clinks of coffee cups. Across from you sits your best friend, visibly anxious. Her eyes dart nervously, and her hands fidget with a napkin. You want to help, but you're unsure how to navigate this emotional minefield without making things worse. This scenario is all too familiar for many young adults who find themselves in the delicate position of supporting loved ones during anxiety episodes. The challenge lies not just in being there but in communicating effectively and offering solace without inadvertently adding to their distress.

Anxiety can turn everyday interactions into complex puzzles that need careful handling. For instance, when a partner feels overwhelmed by sudden changes in plans, it's easy for misunderstandings to escalate into arguments. Friends may withdraw, canceling plans last minute, causing feelings of rejection or confusion. Family members might react with frustration, their well-intentioned advice coming off as dismissive. These scenarios highlight the intricate dance required to maintain harmony in relationships during anxious periods. Without the right communication strategies, these interactions can strain even the strongest bonds, leaving both parties feeling isolated and misunderstood.

This chapter will contain effective communication strategies to navigate these tricky moments. You'll learn the power of active listening and how it can make your loved ones feel genuinely heard. We'll explore methods for expressing your emotions openly and honestly, ensuring that your needs are communicated clearly without escalating tensions. Regular check-ins will be discussed as a way to maintain alignment and trust in your relationships. By establishing clear boundaries and practicing empathy, you'll create a supportive environment where you and your loved ones can thrive, even in the face of anxiety.

# Developing Effective Communication Strategies With Loved Ones During Anxiety

Understanding the dynamics of relationships and communication during anxiety episodes can be transformative. Effective communication strategies with loved ones during these challenging times are not always intuitive, but they are crucial for nurturing supportive connections and alleviating stress.

One of the most impactful ways to support a loved one experiencing anxiety is through active listening. This involves fully concentrating on what the other person is saying without interrupting or planning your response while they're still speaking. Research suggests that when individuals feel genuinely heard, their stress levels can decrease significantly (Bleile, n.d.).

Here are some practical steps to foster active listening:

- Focus entirely on your loved one when they are speaking. Eye contact and nodding can show you are engaged.

- Avoid interrupting. Let them finish their thoughts before you respond.

- Paraphrase or summarize what they said to ensure understanding. Phrases like "What I'm hearing is…" can be very helpful.

- Validate their feelings by acknowledging their emotions, even if you don't fully understand them.

Another critical aspect of effective communication during anxiety is expressing emotions openly and honestly. Using "I" statements rather than accusatory "you" statements can help prevent misunderstandings and resolve conflicts peacefully. For instance, saying, "I feel overwhelmed when plans change suddenly," is often more constructive than "You always change our plans."

Here's a guide to expressing yourself clearly during anxious moments:

- Start with "I" to take ownership of your feelings.

- Clearly state what you're feeling. "I feel stressed" or "I feel anxious" gives specific emotion identifiers.

- Follow up with the reason for your feeling, ensuring it is directly related to an action or event without blaming others. "I feel stressed because I have a lot on my plate right now."

- End with a positive statement to encourage constructive dialogue. "I would appreciate it if we could discuss how to manage these changes."

Regular check-ins are another valuable strategy. Setting aside time to share feelings and update each other on your emotional states can strengthen your emotional bonds and build trust. Think of these check-ins as an opportunity to stay aligned in your relationship, similar to maintaining a garden where regular care promotes healthy growth.

To make the most out of these check-in times:

- Schedule a consistent time that works for both parties. Perhaps once a week in the evening after dinner.

- Keep the atmosphere relaxed and free from distractions. Turn off the TV, put away phones, and focus on each other.

- Use open-ended questions to encourage dialogue. Questions like, "How has your week been?" or "Is there something on your mind you'd like to talk about?" invite richer responses.

- Listen attentively and offer empathetic feedback. Nod, acknowledge their points, and provide supportive comments.

Through these regular interactions, you develop a rhythm of mutual support that reinforces trust and connection.

# Setting Boundaries and Expressing Needs in Relationships While Managing Anxiety

When anxiety creeps into our lives, managing relationships and communication can become a daunting task. However, clearly defined personal boundaries and proper communication can transform these interactions from overwhelming to manageable. Below are four simple steps that can help you define and communicate your boundaries with others.

## *Step 1: Clearly Define Personal Boundaries and Communicate Them*

Setting boundaries is not about creating distance but about safeguarding your emotional well-being. It is a positive, proactive measure to ensure mental peace. Be sure to communicate your limits to your loved ones; it helps manage their expectations and prevents misunderstandings that could lead to stress or resentment.

Here is what you can do to achieve this:

- Reflect on what you need and where you often feel overwhelmed.

- Communicate these needs clearly and assertively to those involved.

- Use "I" statements, such as "I need some alone time when I get home from work to decompress."

- Be consistent with your boundaries and gently remind others if they forget or overstep.

By thoughtfully setting and sticking to personal boundaries, you create a safe space for yourself to recharge, which ultimately benefits everyone involved.

## Step 2: Assertively Express Needs and Seek Support When Necessary

It's essential to be proactive about your emotional needs. Expressing what you need doesn't make you demanding; it signifies that you value self-care. Assertiveness is key here—neither aggressive nor passive, but firm and respectful.

Here is what you can do to express your needs assertively:

- Identify what you genuinely need for your well-being.

- Choose an appropriate time and place to discuss these needs.

- Frame your needs positively. For example, "I need your support by helping to reduce loud noises at home during my anxiety episodes."

- Practice active listening when the other person responds, showing that you respect their perspective too.

By doing so, you're practicing self-care and also inviting your loved ones to understand and support you effectively. This creates a mutually respectful environment.

## *Step 3: Negotiate Compromises and Find Win-Win Solutions in Relationships*

Anxiety can strain relationships, but approaching conflicts with a collaborative mindset eases tension. Don't just think about what you need; consider the other person's perspective. Finding compromises can turn potential points of contention into opportunities for cooperation and closeness.

For instance, if you and your partner disagree about social activities, talk openly about your feelings. Maybe you can agree to dedicate one night a week to socializing while the rest are quieter evenings. This kind of negotiation shows flexibility and willingness to meet halfway, reducing the stress that rigid expectations can create.

## *Step 4: Recognize When to Step Back and Take Space for Self-Care*

There are times when stepping back and taking some personal space becomes crucial. This isn't about avoiding responsibilities or people; it's about recognizing your limits and respecting them.

Here is what you can do to ensure you take necessary space:

- Pay attention to signs of burnout, such as irritation, fatigue, or feeling overwhelmed.

- Plan periods of relaxation throughout your day or week.

- Communicate your need for space to those around you before you're at your breaking point. For example, say, "I'm feeling very overwhelmed right now. I need about an hour to myself to recharge."

Remember that taking a break doesn't mean you're failing; it means giving yourself the chance to return stronger and more resilient. Your emotional well-being always comes first.

As young adults navigating the varying stresses of life, understanding how to set boundaries and articulate our needs is paramount. By doing so, we not only protect our mental health but also pave the way for healthier and more fulfilling relationships. Implementing these practices daily can make a significant difference in managing anxiety and promoting a balanced lifestyle.

Next time you feel anxiety creeping in, remember these steps: define your boundaries, express your needs assertively, seek out compromises, and don't hesitate to take space when required. Practice makes perfect, and each step you take toward assertive communication and boundary-setting is a step toward greater emotional resilience.

# Exploring How Anxiety Can Impact Different Types of Relationships

Recognizing the unique dynamics of romantic relationships, friendships, and family connections can help navigate anxiety triggers more effectively. Anxiety doesn't manifest uniformly across all relationship types; each has its unique set of challenges and intricacies.

The desire for mutual understanding and support can make anxiety particularly pronounced here. Partners may feel overwhelmed by an anxious partner's need for constant reassurance or their tendency to self-silence (Global Counseling Solutions, PLLC, 2022). Friends, on the other hand, might misinterpret these behaviors as disinterest or aloofness. At the same time, family members might struggle with feelings of helplessness or frustration when they witness a loved one grappling with worry.

Understanding how anxiety may manifest differently in various relationships can aid in tailoring communication strategies and support mechanisms. Romantic partners, for example, may notice their significant other exhibiting excessive reassurance-seeking behaviors, constantly needing validation about the status and future of the relationship. Meanwhile, friends might observe patterns of avoidance or withdrawal, where the anxious person cancels plans frequently or isolates themselves socially (Global Counseling Solutions, PLLC, 2022). Families may encounter situations where the person experiencing anxiety becomes irritable or unreasonably fearful about daily routines and interactions

Tailor communication strategies to address manifestations appropriately. In romantic relationships, this could mean establishing clear lines of communication and consistent reassurance practices while balancing personal space. Friendships could involve creating safe spaces where an anxious individual feels comfortable expressing their fears without judgment. Families might benefit from setting up regular check-ins where everyone can voice their concerns and feelings openly. Tailoring these strategies ensures that each relationship type receives specific attention, promoting a more supportive and understanding environment.

Identifying triggers specific to each type of relationship can guide personalized coping strategies and enhance emotional resilience. In romantic relationships, triggers might revolve around trust and intimacy issues. A forgotten promise or a slight delay in response time can escalate anxiety. Friends might trigger you through perceived neglect or lack of reciprocity. Family members, often bound by shared history, might unknowingly touch-sensitive nerves related to past experiences or expectations.

When seeking to learn more about your triggers in each relationship, follow these steps:

- First, identify specific incidents that consistently trigger anxiety within each relationship.

- Second, communicate openly about these triggers with those involved, aiming for a mutual understanding.

- Third, develop personal coping strategies such as deep-breathing exercises or mindfulness techniques to employ when faced with these triggers.

- Fourth, work together to create a supportive environment that acknowledges and respects these triggers, fostering a culture of patience and empathy.

Cultivating empathy and understanding toward loved ones' responses to anxiety can promote mutual support and strengthen relationships. Empathy involves putting oneself in another's shoes and attempting to understand their feelings and reactions. When a loved one struggles, their reactions—whether it be irritability, withdrawal, or over-dependence—are often not personal attacks but manifestations of their internal battle.

In engaging with loved ones' anxiety, active listening becomes crucial. Often, just being there and providing a listening ear can significantly ease their burden. Additionally, educating oneself about mental health and its impacts can go a long way. Understanding the science—how it affects the brain and body—can demystify some of the seemingly irrational behaviors, fostering a more accepting and supportive stance.

Awareness of how anxiety impacts different relationships allows for targeted strategies to maintain connection and communication during challenging times. It's like having a toolkit filled with customized tools for each type of relationship. These tools help manage worry and strengthen the bond between individuals.

In summary, recognizing the specific dynamics of romantic relationships, friendships, and family connections provides a clearer path to navigating anxiety triggers. Tailoring communication strategies ensures that each relationship type gets the appropriate support, fostering understanding and compassion. Identifying specific triggers helps in developing personalized coping strategies and enhancing emotional resilience. Most importantly, cultivating empathy and understanding toward loved ones' responses promotes mutual support and strengthens relationships. By adopting these approaches, we can maintain and even deepen our connections, transforming anxiety episodes from periods of tension into opportunities for growth and bonding.

# Strengthening Relationships Through Effective Communication and Empathy

In reflecting on the dynamics of relationships and communication during anxiety episodes, we've explored various strategies to enhance understanding and connection with loved ones. From practicing active listening to expressing emotions openly, setting aside time for regular check-ins, and establishing clear boundaries, these approaches aim to foster supportive environments that alleviate stress and build trust.

Returning to the essence of our journey, we recognize how vital it is to feel genuinely heard and understood during moments of panic. Active listening, which involves giving our full attention without interruptions, creates a sanctuary where anxious thoughts can be expressed freely. This attentive presence not only calms the person experiencing anxiety but also solidifies the emotional bond between individuals.

Currently, embracing open and honest expression of feelings continues to stand out as a cornerstone for managing anxiety within relationships. Using "I" statements to express one's emotions reduces defensiveness and promotes healthier, more constructive dialogues. For many young adults, mastering this form of communication can transform potential conflicts into opportunities for deeper mutual understanding and empathy.

As we conclude this chapter, consider that every compassionate exchange is a step toward deeper connections and emotional growth. Embrace the journey of understanding and empathy, knowing that each effort you make to communicate effectively during anxious times builds a stronger, more resilient tapestry of relationships. We aren't just managing anxiety through compassion and active listening—we're fostering an environment of mutual respect and enduring support.

In the next chapter, we will examine two anxiety-busting techniques: self-awareness and reflection.

Chapter 5:

# The Power of Self-Awareness

# and Reflection

Today's fast-paced world has no shortage of stressors—be it hectic workdays, social pressures, or personal conflicts. These challenges often translate to restless nights and anxious minds for young adults. Take Emma, a college student juggling part-time jobs and heavy coursework. Her anxiety peaks right before exams, making it hard to concentrate. Or consider Jack, who struggles to maintain emotional stability due to his overwhelming job responsibilities. These situations highlight a common problem: A disconnect between our busy lives and the need for inner peace. The relentless pace often leaves us feeling frazzled and emotionally drained, increasing our vulnerability to anxiety.

This chapter delves into practical strategies to harness self-awareness and reflection for better emotional well-being. Integrating these practices into your daily routine will create a sanctuary of calm within yourself, available whenever you need it. Additionally, you'll discover how daily reflection through activities like journaling can deepen your self-awareness and emotional intelligence. Together, these tools offer positive alternatives to address anxiety and nurture emotional health, setting the stage for a more balanced and serene life.

# Enhancing Self-Awareness Through Daily Reflection

Self-awareness means knowing oneself deeply. It's like looking in a mirror where you see all your strengths, weaknesses, emotions, and thoughts laid out before you. By truly understanding yourself, you can navigate life's challenges more efficiently and make better decisions. Being self-aware helps you understand why you react in certain ways to different situations. It allows you to recognize patterns in your behavior, thoughts, and emotions. For example, if you know you get angry in traffic, you can work on managing your feelings and finding healthier ways to cope. In this section, we will look at various ways to build and strengthen self-awareness so you can feel more in control of your thoughts, feelings, and actions.

## *Embrace Journaling*

Writing down your thoughts can serve as a mirror reflecting your inner world. It helps break down complex emotions and identify patterns that might be contributing to your anxiety. Journaling involves deeper introspection of your emotional triggers and responses than just keeping a diary.

- Begin by setting aside a quiet time each day—maybe in the morning or before bed. Use this time to jot down significant events of the day, focusing on moments that triggered strong emotions.

- Describe not just what happened but also how it made you feel. Be honest about your emotions, whether they are positive or negative.

- Over time, review your entries. Look for recurring themes or triggers. This could help you understand deep-seated issues driving your anxiety.

By embracing journaling, you give your mind a space to process these experiences rather than letting them fester subconsciously (Bailey & Rehman, 2022). Reflective writing allows you to take control, turn vague feelings into tangible words, and better manage your emotional landscape.

## Set Aside Dedicated Time for Introspection

Daily introspection isn't about overthinking every little detail of your life but creating a structured time to reflect and self-assess. Understanding yourself on a deeper level empowers you to handle stress better.

- Choose a specific part of your day when you won't be disturbed. Consistency is key, so making this a daily habit will enhance its effectiveness.

- During your introspective session, ask yourself open-ended questions like "What was the biggest challenge I faced today?" or "How did I respond to stress, and why?"

- Reflect deeply on your answers without judgment. The goal is to understand, not criticize.

This form of introspection can reveal hidden aspects of your behavior and thought processes, helping you make more informed decisions in the future. Remember, the aim is to deepen your self-understanding, enabling you to navigate life's challenges more gracefully.

## Use Reflective Questioning

Reflective questioning pushes you to explore the roots of your beliefs and attitudes. By challenging negative thoughts, you can gradually cultivate a more positive outlook.

- Start by identifying a troubling thought. Write it down.

- Next, ask yourself why you believe this thought. What evidence supports it? Is there any evidence against it?

- Consider alternative perspectives. How would someone else view this situation? Could there be other explanations?

- Finally, reframe the negative thought into something more balanced and constructive.

For instance, if you think, "I always mess things up," challenge it by asking, "Is that true? Can I think of times when I succeeded?" Reflect on past achievements to counteract this negative narrative. This technique helps dismantle harmful beliefs and replace them with healthier, more balanced views (Davis & Hayes, 2012).

## *Practice Gratitude Journaling*

Gratitude journaling is a transformative way to shift focus from what's wrong in your life to what's going well. Fostering resilience starts with recognizing and appreciating positive experiences, no matter how small.

- Each day, write down at least three things you're grateful for. These don't have to be monumental; even small joys like a sunny day or a comforting conversation count.

- Reflect briefly on why you appreciate these things. How do they add value to your life?

- Whenever possible, express your gratitude to those involved. If someone did something kind, let them know—you'll likely brighten their day and strengthen your social bonds.

Regular gratitude practices can dramatically improve your mood and outlook on life. This simple yet powerful exercise builds mental resilience, helping you to bounce back from setbacks and view challenges through a more optimistic lens (Sutton, 2016).

Regular reflection can be a refuge in the storm of anxiety, providing clarity and fostering emotional regulation. By journaling, dedicating time for introspection, using reflective questioning, and practicing gratitude, we can achieve greater self-awareness and compassion. These practices empower us to recognize our emotional responses and handle triggers more effectively.

Through this journey of self-discovery and emotional regulation, remember that the ultimate objective is not perfection but progress. It's about moving toward a state where your emotional well-being takes precedence, guiding you to a more fulfilling, balanced life.

## Increasing Present-Moment Awareness With Mindfulness Meditation

Imagine this: you're sitting in a quiet room, your mind whirling from the chaos of everyday life. Anxious thoughts race through your mind like a storm that just won't quit. This is where mindfulness meditation can be a game-changer—a tool to foster a sense of calm and detachment from those pesky thoughts.

Mindfulness meditation encourages us to become observers of our own minds. By observing your thoughts without getting caught up in their narrative, you cultivate a sense of detachment. This doesn't mean disconnecting entirely from reality; instead, it's about recognizing that anxious thoughts are transient and don't define who you are.

Here's how to deepen your connection to the present moment:

- Focus on your breath as it naturally flows in and out. Notice the coolness of the air as you inhale and the warmth as you exhale.

- Pay attention to the sensation of your body touching the chair or floor. Feel the weight of your hands resting on your lap.

- If your mind wanders—and it will—that's okay. Gently guide your attention back to these present-moment sensations.

This practice works because our breath and bodily sensations are always present. By anchoring ourselves to what's happening right here, right now, we distance ourselves from the anxiety that arises when we dwell on past regrets or future worries.

## *Use Mindfulness Techniques to Create Space Between Stimuli and Responses*

Mindfulness techniques, such as meditation and deep breathing exercises, can effectively create space between stimuli and responses. Practicing mindfulness can cultivate a heightened awareness of your thoughts, feelings, and bodily sensations in the present moment. This increased awareness allows you to observe your reactions to various stimuli without immediately reacting to them. For example, practicing mindfulness can help you pause before responding when confronted with a stressful situation at work, enabling you to choose a more thoughtful and composed reaction.

Creating a mental pause can make all the difference. Here's how you can apply this:

- Take a deep breath before responding when you notice a stressor—like criticism from a colleague or a sudden problem.

- Use this brief pause to check in with your body. Are your shoulders tense? Is your jaw clenched? Relax these areas.

- Ask yourself if there's another way to interpret the situation. For instance, could your colleague's comment be coming from a place of concern rather than criticism?

Creating this space between stimulus and response allows you to choose a reaction that aligns with your values and long-term goals rather than acting out of immediate emotional impulses.

As a young adult navigating the complexities of modern life, these practices offer a sanctuary of inner peace and resilience. So why not give it a try? The next time you find yourself caught in an anxious whirlwind, remember that your breath is always with you, ready to anchor you in the present moment. Embrace this simple yet profound practice, and let it guide you toward a life of greater ease and emotional well-being.

# Promoting Positivity and Resilience With Gratitude Practices

Cultivating a daily gratitude practice by reflecting on small moments of joy, connection, or accomplishment can truly transform your emotional landscape. You might wonder how to start this practice amidst the hustle and bustle of everyday life. It begins with making a conscious choice to pause and notice those fleeting moments that often go unnoticed—like the warmth of a morning sunbeam hitting your face, a sincere "thank you" from a colleague, or completing a task you've been procrastinating on.

Here is what you can do to achieve this:

- Start each day with an intention to be mindful of pleasant moments. As you go about your activities, allow yourself to stop briefly when something positive happens and take a moment to appreciate it.

- At the end of the day, reflect back on these moments and acknowledge their impact on your mood and well-being. You could do this while preparing for bed or during a quiet evening moment.

- Incorporate mindfulness techniques such as deep breathing to anchor these moments in your memory, enhancing your overall awareness and appreciation of them.

Expressing appreciation toward oneself, others, and the world around us fosters a mindset of abundance and positivity. This isn't always about grand gestures—often, it's the little acknowledgments that carry the most weight. For instance, recognizing your efforts after a challenging day, thanking a friend for their support, or simply appreciating a beautiful view all contribute to a sense of fullness and contentment.

Here are more tips that you can try:

- Take a few minutes daily to stand before a mirror and verbally list a few things you appreciate about yourself.

This might feel awkward at first, but the verbal reinforcement strengthens self-compassion over time.

- Make it a habit to send a quick message of thanks to someone who has positively impacted your day, no matter how small their act of kindness might seem.

- Develop a routine where you consciously acknowledge the beauty and value in your surroundings. Whether it's nature, architecture, or even the kindness of strangers, letting yourself feel this appreciation contributes to a more positive outlook on life.

Gratitude can also be a powerful tool to reframe challenging situations and find silver linings, even in difficult times. When adversity hits, it's natural to focus on what's going wrong.

However, shifting your perspective to recognize any positive aspects can profoundly impact your resilience and emotional health. The act of finding something to be thankful for, even if it's just the strength to get through another day, can help you navigate through tough periods.

Creating a gratitude journal to document blessings and experiences that evoke gratitude reinforces positive emotions. Research shows that maintaining a gratitude journal can lead to better mental health by training your brain to focus on positive aspects of your life (Brown & Wong, 2017). This practice doesn't just capture happy moments; it solidifies them into your memory, making it easier to draw strength and comfort from them later.

Here is what you can do to achieve this:

- Choose a time of day, preferably before bed, to jot down a few things you're grateful for. This could range from significant events to everyday comforts.

- Try including why you are grateful for these things or experiences and how they affect your life. Understanding the 'why' deepens your appreciation.

- Review your entries periodically to see patterns in what brings you joy and comfort. These reflections can provide insights into areas of your life that continuously nourish your well-being.

By practicing these gratitude exercises, anxiety-inducing thoughts can shift to focus more on the positive aspects of life, enhancing resilience and fostering emotional well-being. Shifting from a habit of dwelling on stressors to actively seeking out and acknowledging moments of gratitude doesn't negate life's challenges but provides a balanced approach to mental health. According to research, gratitude practices can literally change the way our brains function, steering us away from toxic emotions such as resentment and envy and toward healthier patterns of thinking (Uclahealth, 2023).

Incorporating gratitude into your daily routine creates a ripple effect beyond personal benefits. It strengthens your social relationships by making you more appreciative of others and encouraging a supportive and empathetic community around you. This concept aligns with the "find-remind-bind" theory, suggesting that gratitude helps identify, appreciate, and maintain valuable relationships (Pratt, 2022).

Cultivating gratitude is not just a feel-good exercise—it's a transformative practice supported by a wealth of research indicating its broad-spectrum benefits. From psychological boosts like increased happiness and reduced depression to physical improvements like better heart health and enhanced sleep quality, adopting gratitude practices can significantly improve your overall well-being. Implementing these steps consistently will help you harness the full power of gratitude, making it an invaluable tool in managing anxiety and fostering emotional resilience.

## Embracing a Calmer, More Reflective Life

It's important to acknowledge that every individual's journey with anxiety and emotional well-being is unique. What works for one person might not resonate with another. Therefore, it's crucial to approach these self-awareness and reflection practices with an open mind and a willingness to explore what best suits your needs. Some readers might find immediate relief through journaling, while others might discover profound changes through mindfulness meditation. The beauty of these techniques lies in their flexibility and adaptability to individual preferences and lifestyles.

On a broader scale, embracing these practices can significantly affect our collective well-being. As more individuals incorporate meditation and reflection into their lives, we collectively move toward a society that values mental health and emotional resilience. This shift can lead to stronger, more supportive communities where empathy and understanding prevail over stress and anxiety.

In this ever-changing world, finding moments of stillness and self-awareness is more important than ever. Allow these practices to guide you toward a life rich in emotional well-being and resilience. Embrace the journey, trust the process, and know that each mindful breath, each moment of introspection, and each expression of gratitude is a step toward a more fulfilling and centered life.

In the next chapter, we will explore practical action steps to confront and reduce anxiety triggers.

Chapter 6:

# Overcoming Anxiety Triggers

Have you ever found yourself feeling inexplicably tense while waiting in line or attending a gathering? That tightness in your chest, the racing thoughts—these are moments many of us know too well. Anxiety can sneak up on us when we least expect it, turning everyday situations into overwhelming challenges. However, what if I told you there's a method to not only anticipate these triggers but also manage them effectively? By understanding and addressing these triggers, you can take back control and navigate life with greater ease.

Anxiety often stems from specific situations that consistently trigger stress responses. It might be a job interview that leaves you sleepless or a crowded room that sends your heart racing. These scenarios aren't just random occurrences; they are identifiable events that evoke a predictable emotional response. For instance, you may notice physical symptoms like sweating or a pounding heart whenever you have to speak in public. Emotionally, this could manifest as feelings of dread or frustration. Recognizing these patterns is crucial because it allows you to see that your feelings inexplicable forces—they have discernible causes you can address.

In this chapter, we'll explore effective strategies for identifying, assessing, and overcoming these triggers. You will learn how to create a personalized list of your triggers and develop a proactive action plan tailored to each one. We'll delve into techniques such as deep breathing, visualization, and mindfulness to help you manage anxiety on the spot. Moreover, we'll discuss the importance of self-reflection and adapting your coping mechanisms as you evolve. By the end of this chapter, you'll have a toolkit of strategies designed to help you face life's anxious moments with resilience and confidence.

## Creating a Personalized Anxiety Trigger List and Action Plan

Creating a personalized anxiety trigger list and action plan can be a game-changer for effective management. Let's start with the first step, which is developing a list of specific situations or events that consistently trigger these reactions.

Begin by taking a moment to reflect on various times in your life when you've felt anxious. Write down each situation or event that consistently results in those uncomfortable feelings. Make sure not to rush through this process; give yourself the space to think deeply about these triggers. Keep a journal, and whenever you encounter a new situation that makes you feel anxious, add it to your list.

Moving forward, identify common patterns or themes among your triggers to enhance self-awareness. Are there specific types of social settings that unsettle you? Perhaps they relate to situations where you lack control or certainty. Recognizing these patterns helps you understand that your anxiety isn't random; it has discernible triggers, making it easier to manage.

Once you've identified your triggers, the next step is to create a proactive action plan with coping strategies tailored to each trigger.

This plan will serve as your personal toolkit, helping you navigate stressful scenarios more efficiently. Here's how you can get started:

- Begin by selecting one of your identified anxiety triggers.

- Brainstorm a series of coping strategies that could be effective for this particular trigger. For example, if public speaking makes you anxious, you might practice deep breathing exercises, positive visualization, or even join a supportive group like Toastmasters to improve your skills.

- Make sure to test these coping strategies in low-pressure settings before using them in more significant situations.

- Always have a backup strategy. If deep breathing doesn't calm you, maybe focusing on an object in the room or repeating a calming mantra will help. By having multiple strategies at your disposal, you increase your chances of finding relief when faced with anxiety-inducing situations.

It's also vital to regularly update and revise your trigger list and action plan as you gain insights into your anxiety patterns. As you grow and change, so do your triggers and coping mechanisms.

What worked for you last year might not be as effective now, so continually reassess and adapt.

- Periodically review your trigger list. Add any new triggers that you've discovered and remove those that no longer cause anxiety.

- Similarly, examine your coping strategies. Identify what's working well and what may need adjustment. Don't hesitate to incorporate new techniques you come across through research or recommendations from others.

- Use a journal to track your progress. Documenting your experiences allows you to see how far you've come and understand areas where you still need improvement.

Increased self-awareness through trigger identification aids tremendously in effective management. When you know what sets off your anxiety, you regain a sense of control over your life. Instead of being blindsided by sudden feelings of dread or panic, you'll be prepared. You'll recognize your body's cues and initiate your pre-planned coping strategies, steering yourself back to a state of calm and equilibrium.

This approach is rooted in empirical evidence. Research consistently shows that self-awareness and tailored coping mechanisms can significantly reduce anxiety levels (Gordon, 2023). When you understand the source and apply well-researched strategies, you empower yourself to handle stressors more effectively.

Remember, to approach this task with kindness toward yourself. Anxiety can often feel overwhelming, but it's crucial to acknowledge your efforts and progress, no matter how small they might seem. This journey isn't about eliminating anxiety entirely but about managing it in a way that it no longer controls your life.

Engage with this process wholeheartedly, knowing that each step you take brings you closer to mastering your anxiety. Seek support when needed, whether from friends, family, or mental health professionals. They can offer valuable insights and encouragement, reinforcing your efforts to maintain your mental well-being.

# Implementing Exposure Therapy Techniques for Gradual Desensitization to Triggers

When grappling with anxiety, particularly in our fast-paced lives, the triggers can often feel overwhelming. But with a methodical approach, it's entirely possible to navigate through these anxious moments and come out stronger on the other side. One powerful strategy is exposure therapy—a gradual immersion into what scares us to help lessen the fear over time.

Starting this journey requires careful planning. Begin with the least intense triggers before moving toward the more daunting ones. Think of it like climbing a mountain; you wouldn't start at the peak without acclimatizing first. Gradually introducing yourself to these situations in controlled settings builds resilience without being overwhelmed. For example, if speaking in public causes anxiety, you might start by practicing in front of a mirror, then progress to a small group of friends, and eventually toward larger audiences.

Here's how you can do this effectively:

- Identify your specific anxiety triggers and rank them based on their intensity.

- Start with the least intense trigger. Engage with it in a safe environment until it becomes less distressing.

- Gradually expose yourself to more challenging triggers, ensuring each step feels manageable.

As you're working through exposure, practicing relaxation techniques is crucial. These techniques help manage the physical symptoms of anxiety, making the experience more bearable. Imagine you're about to face one of your triggers: your heart may race, your palms may sweat, or your muscles may tense up. Deep breathing, progressive muscle relaxation, or mindfulness meditation can significantly reduce these symptoms.

During exposure, incorporate relaxation:

- Take slow, deep breaths, inhaling through your nose and exhaling through your mouth.

- Practice progressive muscle relaxation by tensing and releasing different muscle groups.

- Use mindfulness to stay present, acknowledging your feelings without judgment.

Tracking progress along this journey is another essential component. Monitoring your experiences provides tangible evidence of improvement, which can be incredibly motivating. It's easy to feel stuck when we don't see immediate change, but recording small victories can highlight significant strides over time.

Keep a journal detailing each exposure session to track your progress, noting emotions, physical sensations, and any improvements. You can also rate your anxiety levels before, during, and after each session to visualize your progress. Finally, reflect on these entries regularly to celebrate milestones and identify areas needing more focus.

Of course, seeking support from a therapist or trusted individual ensures this process remains safe and effective. A mental health professional can provide tailored guidance and encouragement, helping adjust strategies as needed. They offer an objective view, spotting potential pitfalls and suggesting adjustments that might not be apparent otherwise.

Gradual exposure isn't just about diving headfirst into our fears; it's about learning to navigate them with confidence. By starting small, using relaxation techniques, tracking progress, and seeking support, we can desensitize ourselves to anxiety triggers and reclaim control over our lives.

The science behind exposure therapy supports its efficacy across various forms of anxiety. According to the American Psychological Association (APA), facing feared objects or situations within a controlled and safe environment helps reduce fear and decrease avoidance (*Exposure Therapy*, n.d.). This kind of gradual confrontation assists in habituation, where repeated exposure leads to a decrease in anxiety responses.

Another significant aspect is emotional processing. Through consistent exposure, individuals can develop new, realistic beliefs about their fears, diminishing the power these anxieties hold over them (*Exposure Therapy*, n.d.). This shift is empowering, enabling people to see themselves as capable of handling anxiety-inducing situations.

Remember, the end goal of exposure therapy is not to eliminate anxiety completely but to reduce its impact on daily life. It fosters resilience, boosts self-efficacy, and encourages healthier coping mechanisms. Whether it's a phobia, social anxiety, or PTSD, the structured approach of exposure therapy offers a pathway to manage and overcome these challenges.

Let's ground this discussion in an example many might relate to—fear of public speaking. This skill is often indispensable but equally intimidating for a young adult entering the professional world.

Imagine you have a presentation coming up. To tackle this with exposure therapy, you could:

- Begin by speaking aloud alone, practicing your material in front of a mirror.

- Progress to presenting in front of a friend or family member who can provide constructive feedback.

- Move on to delivering your talk to a small group, perhaps a study group or workshop, before taking on larger settings like a classroom or office meeting.

Throughout these stages, employ relaxation techniques like deep breathing to stay calm. Track your feelings and physiological responses to measure progress. Share your fears and achievements with a supportive mentor or peer, maintaining an open dialogue about your experiences.

This personalized, step-by-step progression enables you to confront the fear of public speaking systematically, reducing anxiety incrementally and making each subsequent challenge less daunting than the last.

# Developing a Resilience Toolkit for Managing Unexpected Triggers Effectively

Unpredictability can be our worst enemy when it comes to anxiety. We can't always anticipate when a curveball will come our way, but having a resilience toolkit ready can make all the difference. Developing such a toolkit involves a combination of varied tools, continuous practice, seeking feedback, and embracing flexibility.

First, include a variety of tools and techniques in your toolkit to address different types of triggers. The nature of triggers can vary widely — from work-related stressors to social anxieties. Each requires its own specific approaches. So, your toolkit needs to include a range of exercises like breathing exercises, visualization techniques, cognitive restructuring techniques, and physical activity like yoga to reduce anxiety levels.

By equipping yourself with these diverse strategies, you ensure that you're prepared no matter what comes your way.

Next, practice relaxation and mindfulness exercises regularly to strengthen your emotional resilience. Building these habits into your daily routine can create a solid foundation of calmness and stability. To commit to these habits, start small. For instance, you can initially start with a 5-10 minute meditation, take short mindfulness breaks in between your tasks, and experiment with different forms of mindfulness practices like progressive muscle relaxation, mindful eating, mindful walking, and loving-kindness meditations.

Regular practice fosters an internal environment that's more resistant to anxiety triggers. It's like building a mental muscle—the more you work at it, the stronger it becomes.

Another critical aspect is to seek feedback from others about the effectiveness of your toolkit and make necessary adjustments. Sometimes, we might not see our blind spots or recognize when a tool isn't working as intended. Engaging friends, family, or professionals can offer valuable perspectives.

Here's what you can do:

- Share your experiences with trusted individuals and ask if they notice any changes in your behavior or mood.

- Discuss tools and techniques with a therapist who can provide expert advice and fine-tune your strategies.

- Join support groups where you can share and learn from others' experiences.

- Keep a journal of your anxiety management efforts and review it with someone who can provide constructive feedback.

This feedback loop ensures that your toolkit evolves and remains effective over time.

Flexibility and adaptability are key in utilizing your toolkit based on the evolving nature of triggers. Life is dynamic, and so should be your approach to managing anxiety. What worked yesterday might need tweaking today. Embrace change and be willing to modify your toolkit as needed.

A well-equipped resilience toolkit empowers individuals to respond effectively to unforeseen triggers. Remember, overcoming anxiety is not about eliminating all stress or fear; instead, it's about developing the strength and skills to face these challenges head-on. By incorporating varied tools, practicing regularly, seeking outside perspectives, and staying flexible, you'll build a robust system of support that sustains you through life's inevitable ups and downs.

Take Robert, for instance. He once struggled immensely with social anxiety. Once he started using a combination of deep breathing techniques and cognitive restructuring, he found himself managing social gatherings better. He practiced daily mindfulness, making him more present and less reactive in stressful situations. Feedback from his therapist helped him refine his approach, ensuring he wasn't falling back into old patterns. Now, Robert adapts his methods as his social circles evolve, maintaining control over his anxiety irrespective of new scenarios.

Having coping strategies readily available enhances resilience in managing anxiety triggers. The more you practice these techniques, the more adept you'll become at handling stressful situations. Remember, there's no one-size-fits-all approach to coping—it's about figuring out what works best for you. Incorporating these practices into your daily life can empower you to face anxious moments with greater confidence and composure. Life will always throw curveballs, but with a solid set of tools at your disposal, you'll be better equipped to handle whatever comes your way. So take a deep breath, visualize that peaceful place, ground yourself in the now, listen to your favorite tune, lace up your sneakers for a brisk walk, and remind yourself that you've got this.

## Empowering Yourself Against Anxiety

Throughout this chapter, we've delved into the intricate process of identifying, assessing, and overcoming triggers in various life situations. Creating a personalized anxiety trigger list and action plan serves as the foundation for understanding what sparks your anxious feelings. Breaking down these triggers into physical sensations, emotional responses, and environmental factors equips you with vital insights. Gradually, this becomes an empowering step toward recognizing patterns that may have once seemed random.

In exploring exposure therapy, we uncovered the value of facing fears in a controlled, progressive manner. Starting small and building up can gradually diminish the power these anxieties hold over you. Coupling this approach with mindfulness and relaxation techniques further aids in managing the stress physically manifested during these moments. Practicing these methods regularly nurtures emotional resilience, transforming how you handle future triggers.

Equally important is developing a resilience toolkit tailored to manage unexpected triggers effectively. Including a variety of tools ensures that you're prepared for diverse scenarios. Seeking feedback and being open to adjustments keeps your strategies relevant and effective over time. Embracing flexibility enhances your ability to adapt, making it easier to navigate through life's unpredictable nature.

As we conclude this chapter, reflect on the progress you've made and the tools you've gathered. Consider how integrating these strategies can reshape your relationship with anxiety, allowing for moments of clarity even amidst turmoil. This proactive approach not only empowers you but also inspires those around you to embark on their own paths toward mental well-being. Remember, each small victory contributes to a larger tapestry of resilience, guiding you through life with confidence and grace. So, take a deep breath, embrace the journey, and trust in your capacity to overcome.

In the next chapter, we will discuss the importance and impact of lifestyle changes in helping you manage anxiety levels.

Chapter 7:

# Understanding the Influence of Lifestyle Changes on Anxiety Levels

Imagine waking up in the morning feeling completely refreshed and ready to tackle the day ahead. You've had a restful night of sleep, eaten a nutritious breakfast, exercised a bit, and are now sipping on some herbal tea while scrolling through your social media feed for the latest updates. It sounds like an ideal scenario, doesn't it? Yet, for many of us, managing these aspects of our lives—diet, exercise, sleep, and digital habits—can be a daily struggle, especially when anxiety seems to be a constant companion.

Anxiety can feel like a sneaky thief that slowly drains your energy and joy. Consider this: you're having a busy day at work or school, constantly checking your smartphone for notifications, grabbing fast food for lunch because you didn't have time to prepare something healthy, skipping your workout because you're too tired, and then struggling to fall asleep because your mind is racing. Each of these habits might seem insignificant on its own, but collectively, they contribute to heightened anxiety levels. For example, consuming too much caffeine or sugar can make you jittery, lack of sleep can make you irritable, and endless scrolling on social media can make you anxious about not measuring up to others.

In this chapter, we'll take a closer look at how making small but meaningful lifestyle changes can help manage anxiety. You'll discover the importance of choosing the right foods to nourish both body and mind, the benefits of regular physical activity, the role of quality sleep in maintaining mental health, and how setting boundaries with technology can bring peace. By exploring these elements, you'll gain practical tips on how to incorporate healthier habits into your daily routine, reducing anxiety and enhancing your overall well-being. So, whether you're looking to make a big change or just tweak a few habits, this chapter will offer valuable insights to guide you on your journey to a calmer, happier life.

## The Correlation Between Dietary Patterns and Anxiety Symptoms

When we think about how diet can impact anxiety, it's helpful to imagine our bodies as highly sophisticated machines that need the right fuel to run smoothly. The foods we eat play a significant role in our mental health, and there's plenty of evidence to back this up.

First, let's consider certain foods like whole grains, fruits, and vegetables. These aren't just good for our physical health; they help support mental well-being too. They provide essential nutrients and antioxidants that our brains need to function properly. For instance, whole grains help maintain steady blood sugar levels, which can prevent mood swings and anxiety.

Incorporating these foods into your diet allows you to harness their benefits. Think about starting your day with oatmeal topped with fresh berries or enjoying a lunch packed with leafy greens and a variety of veggies. It's not just about eating healthy; it's about making specific choices that will bolster your mental health over time.

However, not all foods are created equal when it comes to managing anxiety. Excessive intake of caffeine and sugar can lead to heightened anxiety levels. Imagine that jittery feeling you get after drinking one too many cups of coffee—now multiply that by a few times, and you have a recipe for increased anxiety.

Maintaining a balanced diet with sufficient hydration is another cornerstone of reducing anxiety symptoms. Dehydration has been shown to affect mood and energy levels negatively, so ensuring you drink plenty of water is crucial. Simple steps like carrying a water bottle with you can make staying hydrated much easier.

To keep your diet balanced, include a mix of proteins, healthy fats, and complex carbohydrates in your meals. Additionally, make water your go-to beverage and limit sugary drinks and sodas. Eat regular meals to prevent dips in blood sugar levels, which can trigger anxiety. Another important aspect is mindful eating, which involves being conscious of how different foods affect your mood. Practicing mindful eating means paying attention to your body's hunger cues and noticing how you feel before, during, and after eating. This can be incredibly empowering, allowing you to make food choices that enhance your well-being.

Here's how you can practice mindful eating:

- Take time to chew your food thoroughly and savor each bite.

- Notice how different foods make you feel emotionally and physically.

- Avoid distractions like TV or smartphones while eating to focus on your meal fully.

A well-rounded diet doesn't just alleviate anxiety in the short term; it sets the foundation for long-term mental health. Research from Harvard Health suggests that consistently eating well-balanced meals and adequate hydration helps keep mood fluctuations at bay (Naidoo, 2020). Likewise, the Mayo Clinic underscores the importance of complex carbohydrates and protein for maintaining steady energy levels and reducing anxiety symptoms (Sawchuk, 2017).

It's clear that what we eat can significantly impact our mental health. By paying attention to dietary patterns and making informed choices, we can take proactive steps toward reducing our anxiety levels. Remember, it's not about perfection but about making gradual changes that collectively lead to better mental well-being.

On the flip side, avoiding negative habits such as excessive consumption of caffeine or sugary foods can also make a substantial difference. Many people don't realize how much hidden sugar they're consuming daily. Foods such as sauces, dressings, and even some breads contain high amounts of added sugar. Reducing these can help prevent spikes in anxiety levels.

That said, taking these steps might seem daunting at first, but breaking them down into manageable actions can help. Gradually replace one sugary item in your diet with a healthier alternative each week. Moreover, track your caffeine intake and try to reduce it incrementally rather than cutting it out all at once. By leveraging good dietary practices and mindfulness, you equip yourself with tools to manage anxiety better. Incorporating nutritious foods, staying hydrated, and practicing mindful eating can transform your relationship with food and help stabilize your mood.

The goal isn't to follow a rigid set of rules but to find a balance that works for you. As you become more attuned to how different foods affect your anxiety levels, you'll naturally gravitate toward choices that make you feel better mentally and physically. Over time, these small changes add up, substantial improving your overall well-being.

Remember, while diet is an essential piece of the puzzle, it often works best in conjunction with other lifestyle changes like exercise, sleep, and digital habits. Approaching your mental health from a holistic perspective is more likely to find lasting relief from anxiety. And always, if your mental health feels unmanageable, seeking professional advice from a doctor or nutritionist can provide additional support tailored to your needs.

So, next time you're planning your meals or feeling overwhelmed by anxiety, recall the power that lies in the choices you make about what to eat. Each small step toward a healthier diet is a step toward a calmer, more balanced state of mind.

# Benefits of Regular Physical Activity in Reducing Stress and Anxiety

It's fascinating how something as simple as moving your body can have profound effects on your mental health. Let's explore the benefits of regular physical activity in reducing stress and anxiety.

Exercise releases endorphins, those delightful mood lifters that can help combat feelings of anxiety and depression. These tiny neurotransmitters are your body's natural painkillers and stress relievers. Think of them as nature's very own cheerleaders that give you a mental high after a good workout session.

So, what can you do to benefit from endorphins? Finding an exercise routine that you actually enjoy is key. Here's a tip: Pick activities that light you up inside. Maybe it's dancing, jogging, or even a brisk walk in the park. The trick is to engage consistently with something you look forward to. Trust me, when you're enjoying it, you're more likely to stick with it.

Moreover, regular exercise fosters better sleep quality, which plays a crucial role in overall mental health and managing anxiety. When you move your body, you tire yourself out physically, helping you fall asleep faster and achieve deeper, more restorative sleep cycles. Good sleep is like hitting the 'reset' button for your brain, helping you cope better with life's challenges.

If you've been struggling with sleep, incorporating exercise into your daily routine might just be the ticket to those sweet dreams. Start with just a few minutes of moderate activity each day, and gradually increase the duration and intensity. You'll find yourself drifting off more easily and waking up refreshed.

Engaging in regular exercise provides a healthy outlet for stress and tension, reducing the buildup of anxiety. Think about this: When you're stressed, those emotions need a way out. Physical activity can serve as an excellent channel for releasing pent-up energy and frustrations. It's almost like letting steam out of a pressure cooker.

Finally, incorporating both cardio and strength-training exercises into your routine can improve your resilience to stress and enhance overall well-being. Cardio workouts—like running or swimming—get your heart pumping and improve cardiovascular health, whereas strength training builds muscle and boosts metabolism. Together, they create a powerful anti-stress regimen.

To strike a balance, aim for a mix of aerobic and strength exercises. For instance, you could alternate between running one day and lifting weights the next. This combination amps up your physical fitness and strengthens your mental fortitude.

Regular exercise offers a plethora of benefits beyond physical health. It significantly enhances mental well-being by combating anxiety and depression, promoting better sleep, and serving as an effective stress relief mechanism. Find what works for you, remain consistent, and revel in the holistic transformation you'll undergo.

# Importance of Maintaining a Healthy Sleep Routine for Mental Well-Being

Consistent sleep patterns are more than just a routine; they function as the bedrock of our mental well-being. Science backs it up: getting regular, high-quality sleep can help regulate mood, enhance cognitive function, and bolster emotional resilience. This, in turn, reduces susceptibility to anxiety. Just imagine waking up each day feeling refreshed rather than groggy. When you establish a consistent sleep schedule, your body adjusts its internal clock accordingly, leading to better-rested mornings and more productive days.

Here is what you can do to cultivate consistent sleep patterns:

- Strive to wake up and go to bed at the same time every day, even on weekends.

- Avoid napping late in the afternoon, which can disrupt your nighttime sleep.

- Consider using an alarm to wake up and as a reminder to wind down for bed.

Creating a calming bedtime routine signals to your body that it's time to wind down. Picture this: you've had a long day, your mind is racing, and all you want is to find some peace before sleep. A structured bedtime routine can be incredibly grounding. Consistent steps—such as reading a book, taking a warm bath, or practicing mindfulness—can clue your body into the fact that sleep is imminent, helping you to fall asleep more easily and enjoy higher-quality- rest.

Limiting screen time before bed is crucial for improving sleep hygiene and, by extension, mental health. The blue light emitted by screens—from smartphones and computers to TVs—interferes with melatonin production, making it harder to fall asleep. You may think you're unwinding by scrolling through social media or watching a movie, but these activities can actually disrupt your sleep cycle.

To optimize your environment for sleep, consider these steps:

- Store electronic devices away from the bedroom to resist the temptation of late-night scrolling.

- Invest in blackout curtains or an eye mask to block out any disruptive light sources.

- Use apps or device settings to reduce blue light exposure during evening hours.

Prioritizing adequate rest and relaxation isn't just about avoiding burnout—it's essential for managing stress and reducing anxiety. Think about those nights when you've skimped on sleep, only to find yourself frazzled and irritable the next day. Adequate sleep helps the mind process emotions and manage stressful situations more effectively. On a biochemical level, restorative sleep allows the brain to process and sort through the experiences of the day, leaving you better equipped to handle whatever comes next.

The consequences of poor sleep extend beyond simply feeling tired. Chronic sleep deprivation has been linked to increased risks of various health issues, including heart disease, diabetes, and mental health disorders such as anxiety and depression. Adequate sleep plays a pivotal role in emotional regulation and boosting resilience, as it's during sleep that the brain processes and stores emotional information (Suni & Dimitriu, 2024). In short, good sleep hygiene is an indispensable component of overall mental health.

Let's not forget the compelling data backing all these claims. A meta-analysis of randomized controlled trials found that interventions aimed at improving sleep significantly reduced symptoms of anxiety and depression (Scott et al., 2021). Additionally, the U.S. Department of Health and Human Services emphasizes the importance of regular, good-quality sleep for reducing stress, improving mood, and enhancing cognitive functions (*Getting Enough Sleep*, 2024).

Establishing a regular sleep schedule creates a stable foundation for enhanced emotional health. Making sure your sleep environment promotes relaxation can further improve sleep quality, which is pivotal for emotional regulation and building resilience against anxiety. Quality sleep, enriched with consistency and conducive practices, forms the cornerstone of mental well-being.

Sleep might seem like a simple part of everyday life. Still, its effects ripple throughout our mental and physical health, impacting everything from cognitive function to emotional stability. As research continues to underscore the importance of sleep for maintaining mental health, it's evident that these practices aren't just beneficial—they're necessary.

So, if you often find yourself battling anxiety or other mental health challenges, consider taking a closer look at your sleep habits. It could be the first step toward a healthier, happier life. It's time we all started giving sleep the priority it deserves.

# Impact of Excessive Screen Time and Social Media on Anxiety Levels

Many of us have experienced the lure of endless scrolling, binge-watching, or repeated checking of updates. Our screens often monopolize more of our time than we'd like to admit. But what does this mean for our mental health? More specifically, how do excessive screen time and social media usage impact anxiety levels?

The relationship between screen time and anxiety is complex and multifaceted. By diving into the research, we can see a clear connection: too much screen time can amplify feelings of overwhelm. This primarily stems from information overload and constant comparison with others. Social media, while connecting us to friends and news, also bombards us with an overwhelming amount of information. This influx can lead to stress as we try to keep up with the latest trends, news, and updates. Additionally, seeing curated snapshots of others' lives often leads us to compare ourselves unfavorably, resulting in feelings of inadequacy and heightened anxiety (Zhao et al., 2023).

To counter these effects, it's essential to set boundaries around technology use. The idea isn't to abandon our devices entirely but rather to engage with them more mindfully. Taking deliberate breaks, commonly referred to as digital detoxes, can help reduce stress and provide much-needed mental clarity. These breaks give us time to recharge and diminish the constant stimuli from screens.

Here is what you can do in order to achieve this:

- Start by designating specific times during the day when you'll be completely offline. For example, consider limiting screen time during meals or before bedtime.

- Create tech-free zones in your home, such as the dining room or bedroom. This helps create physical separation from screens and fosters a healthier environment.

- Engage in other fulfilling activities during your digital detox, such as reading a book, going for a walk, or simply enjoying some quiet time.

Beyond just taking breaks, it's crucial to re-engage with the offline world. Spending too much time online can lead to social isolation. Instead, nurturing real-life connections can significantly boost our well-being. Participating in community events, catching up with friends face-to-face, or joining clubs and organizations can provide a sense of belonging and alleviate the anxiety caused by excessive digital interactions.

Mindfulness plays a pivotal role in developing a healthier relationship with technology. Practicing mindfulness allows us to become more aware of our habits and their impacts on our mental state. By being intentional about our screen time, we can foster a balance that supports our mental health and lowers anxiety levels.

Here are some practical steps to practice mindfulness with screen time:

- Before reaching for your phone or laptop, take a moment to ask yourself why you're doing it. Is it out of habit, boredom, or necessity?

- Use apps that track your screen time and provide insights into your usage patterns. This can help identify areas where you might need to cut back.

- Incorporate short meditation sessions into your routine. Even a few minutes each day can help center your thoughts and reduce anxiety.

While technology offers countless benefits, it's imperative to recognize its potential drawbacks. Evidence suggests a strong link between excessive screen time and mental health issues like anxiety and depression (Nakshine et al., 2022). Constant exposure to screens can affect sleep patterns, increase stress hormones, and alter brain chemistry. For young adults, whose brains are still developing, this can lead to long-term consequences.

In particular, a study conducted by researchers at Yale and Columbia analyzed over 5,100 children aged 9 and 10. Results showed that those who spent the most time on digital devices were more likely to develop internalizing problems, including anxiety, two years later (Zhao et al., 2023). This underscores the importance of moderating screen time from an early age.

If you're feeling overwhelmed by your digital habits, know that you're not alone. Many people struggle with finding a healthy balance. However, small, consistent changes can make a significant difference. Being mindful of your screen time and setting boundaries doesn't mean cutting yourself off from the digital world; it means reclaiming control over your life and prioritizing your mental health.

Remember, the goal isn't perfection but progress. By incorporating these guidelines and practices into your daily routine, you're taking proactive steps toward reducing anxiety and improving overall well-being. Embrace the power of real-life connections, enjoy offline activities, and approach your screen time with intention and mindfulness. You'll find that by doing so, you're not only fostering a healthier relationship with technology but also paving the way for a more balanced and fulfilling life.

## Integrating Healthy Habits for Anxiety Management

Throughout this chapter, we've explored the profound ways diet, exercise, sleep, and digital habits influence anxiety. By treating our bodies like the sophisticated machines they are, we can ensure they get the right kind of fuel—emotional and physical—to function optimally. Our dietary choices, brimming with whole grains, fruits, and vegetables, play a pivotal role not just in physical health but in stabilizing our mental well-being too. Meanwhile, regular physical activity acts as a powerful antidote to stress, releasing endorphins that uplift our mood and help us cope with life's challenges.

Returning to an earlier statement, it's clear that establishing consistent routines is key. Just as balancing nutritious meals and staying hydrated can lay a strong foundation for mental health, maintaining a regular sleep schedule reinforces emotional stability and resilience against anxiety. Prioritizing restful sleep enables us to wake up refreshed, ready to tackle the day with a clearer mind and steadier heart.

Our current position underscores the importance of mindfulness across all these areas. Mindful eating, moving, sleeping, and screen-time management allow us to navigate life's stressors more effectively. However, it's essential to recognize that putting these practices into action might seem overwhelming initially. It's okay to start small—whether by replacing a sugary snack with a healthier option, incorporating a short walk after meals, or setting boundaries around screen time.

Consider the ripple effects: improved personal habits can lead to better collective mental health. Each small change you make contributes to a larger shift toward a healthier, happier community. As we draw from the wisdom shared in this chapter, remember that this journey isn't about perfection. It's about gradual, sustainable changes that collectively enhance our overall well-being.

I'll leave you with this open-ended thought: What small step can you take today to nourish your body, calm your mind, and foster a healthier relationship with your habits? Reflect on it, act on it, and watch how these mindful choices transform your life's landscape.

In the next chapter, we explore the benefits of immersing yourself in nature, engaging in creative pursuits, and cuddling with your furry pets as part of your anxiety management plan.

Chapter 8:

# Harnessing the Therapeutic Benefits of Nature, Creativity, and Human Connections

In today's fast-paced world, anxiety has become an all-too-common companion for many young adults. The pressures of school, work, and social expectations can often feel overwhelming, leading to feelings of stress. Consider how you might feel after spending hours indoors, hunched over a computer screen, only to step outside and be greeted by the warm embrace of the sun or the gentle sway of trees in the breeze. Similarly, think about the sense of accomplishment and joy that comes from completing a creative project, whether a painting, a knitted scarf, or a short story. Or recall a moment when a shared laugh with friends provided much-needed relief from a stressful situation. These experiences highlight how nature, creativity, humor, and connections help mitigate anxiety and uplift our spirits.

In this chapter, we will delve into the various methods for harnessing these natural therapies to manage anxiety and improve overall well-being. You will learn about the proven benefits of spending time in natural environments, simple yet effective ways to incorporate creativity into your daily routine, the importance of humor in coping with stress, and the profound impact of strong human connections. By exploring each of these elements, you'll discover practical strategies to integrate them into your own life, fostering a more balanced and resilient approach to mental health.

## The Restorative Effects of Natural Environments on Mental Well-Being

Spending time in nature can have remarkable effects on our mental well-being, and abundant evidence supports this notion. Imagine strolling through a dense forest filled with the scent of fresh pine or sitting by a tranquil lake with the sounds of chirping birds in the background. These experiences don't just feel refreshing; they actually help reduce cortisol levels—the hormone most closely associated with stress.

Research has shown that exposure to natural environments decreases cortisol, ultimately resulting in feelings of calm and relaxation (Jimenez et al., 2021). To harness these benefits, consider infusing your routine with moments spent outdoors. Here's how you can do it:

- Start your day with a walk in a nearby park or a green space.

- During lunch breaks, try to find a spot outside to sit quietly for a few minutes.

- On weekends, plan activities like hiking, picnicking, or visiting botanical gardens.

- Even small steps—like incorporating houseplants into your living space—can contribute to lowering those stress levels.

Moreover, nature doesn't just soothe our nerves; it also uplifts our spirits. When we immerse ourselves in natural settings, such as taking long walks in the park or simply basking in the afternoon sun, we often notice a significant improvement in mood. The vibrant colors, varied textures, and calming sounds of nature work synergistically to elevate our overall mental health outcomes. This isn't just anecdotal; data supports the idea that outdoor activities can enhance mood and foster positive emotions (Jimenez et al., 2021).

Getting your mood boost from nature can be incredibly straightforward. You might start by simply going outside for at least 15–20 minutes each day. Morning sunlight is particularly beneficial as it brightens your day and balances the circadian rhythms, setting a positive tone for the rest of the day. If you have access to natural trails or even tree-lined streets, take advantage of them. Each step you take in a natural environment helps to cultivate a more emotionally resilient frame of mind.

The interplay between sunlight, fresh air, and our biological processes also shouldn't be undervalued. Exposure to these natural elements can increase serotonin levels, which play a vital role in maintaining our sense of well-being. Unlike artificial lighting and recycled indoor air, natural sunlight works wonders by catalyzing vitamin D synthesis in our bodies, which in turn aids serotonin production. While this seems like a passive benefit of being outdoors, it actively enhances our mood and sense of balance.

Then, there are mindful practices like gardening or hiking that offer dual benefits—both physical activity and psychological relief. Engaging with nature through these avenues becomes a form of mindfulness, allowing us to disconnect from daily stressors and refocus on the present moment. Gardening, for instance, involves touching the soil, tending to plants, and watching them grow, which can be especially therapeutic. Hiking adds the dimension of physical exertion combined with the immersive experience of traversing diverse landscapes.

For those looking to incorporate these practices into their lives:

- Begin with small gardening projects, even if it's a tiny herb garden on your windowsill.

- Join local hiking groups or clubs, which can provide both social interaction and guidance on the best local trails.

- Dedicate specific times during the week for these activities to build a routine around them.

- Use these opportunities to practice mindfulness by focusing on your surroundings—the texture of leaves, the sound of rustling branches, and the scent of earth.

Immersing oneself in nature offers more than just a temporary escape—it provides a substantial positive impact on mental health. Beyond cortisol reduction and mood enhancement, these experiences act like a reset button for our stressed-out minds and bodies. They instill a sense of tranquility and relaxation that is hard to replicate with any other form of intervention. When we allow ourselves to step away from the hustle and bustle and embrace the natural world, we gain more than just brief moments of respite. We cultivate a sustainable approach to managing anxiety and improving our overall quality of life.

Remember, the goal isn't to overhaul your entire lifestyle overnight. Instead, focus on small, meaningful changes that integrate nature into your daily routine. Whether it's through morning walks, weekend hikes, or tending a little garden, each interaction with nature brings you one step closer to a calmer, happier self. So, lace up those walking shoes, grab a spade, and let the healing power of nature work its magic.

# Integrating Creative Activities Into Daily Routines for Stress Relief

Engaging in creative pursuits such as painting, writing, or crafting can act as outlets for self-expression and emotional release. Just imagine dipping a brush into a brilliant blue and sweeping it across a blank canvas—or perhaps sitting down with a journal, letting your thoughts flow freely onto the page. These activities are more than hobbies; they offer a sanctuary from the stresses of daily life, a moment where the mind can find peace through creation.

When life feels overwhelming, taking the first step toward creativity might seem daunting, but it's simpler than you think.

Here's what you can do to start:

- Choose an activity that excites you: painting, knitting, journaling, or something else.

- Gather your materials so they're always within reach. This makes it easier to begin whenever inspiration strikes.

- Set aside a small, dedicated space where you can work undisturbed.

- Allow yourself to be messy and imperfect—remember, this is about expression, not perfection.

Dedicating even just a few minutes a day to these pursuits can provide a powerful outlet for your emotions, helping you process feelings that might otherwise remain bottled up.

Creative activities allow individuals to focus their attention and redirect negative thoughts, promoting a sense of accomplishment and fulfillment. Think of moments when you're lost in a task, completely absorbed in what you're doing—perhaps arranging flowers, building a model, or composing music. In those moments, negativity seems to dissolve, replaced by a profound concentration and fulfillment.

This process allows you to redirect your negative thoughts into productive, creative energy. As you complete each small project, you'll feel a sense of achievement that boosts your overall well-being.

Participating in artistic endeavors can stimulate the brain's reward pathways, enhancing mood and reducing anxiety levels. When you engage in a creative activity, your brain releases dopamine—a chemical associated with pleasure and reward. This helps create a positive feedback loop where the more you make, the better you feel and the more likely you are to continue creating.

Art provides a wonderful escape, but more than that, it enriches our lives by making us see the world differently. The Journal of Positive Psychology notes that spending time on creative goals during the day is linked with higher activated positive affect, essentially meaning we feel happier and more optimistic (*The Mental Health Benefits of Creativity*, n.d.).

Setting aside dedicated time for creativity can serve as a form of self-care and foster a sense of purpose and joy. Self-care isn't merely about bubble baths and face masks; it's fundamentally about finding what genuinely nurtures your soul. If art brings you joy, then setting aside time for it is an essential self-care practice.

The arts hold incredible healing potential, providing tools that are both accessible and enjoyable. By integrating creative practices into your life, you're not just developing a skill— you're nurturing your spirit, managing stress, enhancing emotional well-being, and fostering a sense of joy and purpose.

So, pick up that paintbrush, pen, or needle, and let creativity become a cornerstone of your self-care routine. Your mind and body will thank you for it.

# The Role of Humor in Coping With Anxiety and Enhancing Mood

When it comes to coping with anxiety, humor often gets overlooked as a powerful tool. Imagine standing in the middle of a crowded room, your heart racing, palms sweaty, feeling utterly overwhelmed. Now, picture someone breaking that tension with a perfectly timed joke. You chuckle, and suddenly, the weight lifts a little. Laughter does that—it triggers the release of endorphins, those wonderful chemicals our bodies produce that make us feel good. It's like nature's way of saying, "Hey, chill out, you've got this."

Humor serves as more than just a momentary distraction; it can act as a coping mechanism too. For example, let's say you had a rough day at work. Instead of letting it consume you, try to find the humor in the situation. Maybe spin a funny story out of the mishaps you experienced. This not only reframes the situation but also helps maintain a positive outlook.

Here is what you can do:

- Start by acknowledging the stressful situation.

- Look for something light-hearted within that context.

- Turn it into a humorous anecdote or a punchline.

- Share it with someone who would appreciate it.

Laughter shared with others can also strengthen social bonds. Think about those belly laughs shared with friends over inside jokes or the giggles during silly moments with family. Sharing these light-hearted moments provides a sense of connection and camaraderie. It reminds us that we are not alone and that others share in our experiences and emotions.

Here's how you can incorporate humor into your relationships:

- Tell a funny story about your day.

- Share memes or videos that made you laugh.

- Create an environment where laughter is encouraged and welcomed.

Incorporating humor into daily interactions brings a sense of lightness and perspective to stressful experiences. Imagine you're stuck in traffic, late for an appointment. Instead of stewing in frustration, play a funny podcast or think of a humorous scenario involving the absurdity of the situation. These small shifts won't change the external circumstances but will definitely alter how you perceive and react to them.

The beauty of humor lies in its simplicity and accessibility. A shared joke or funny anecdote has the power to lighten even the heaviest of moods. Plus, it fosters resilience by helping us detach from the immediate stressors and look at the bigger picture with a smile.

Importantly, research supports the therapeutic effects of humor. According to findings published by The Jed Foundation, laughter increases the production of endorphins while reducing stress hormones like cortisol (Fleming, n.d.). This dual action creates an emotional buffer, making us feel happier and less anxious almost immediately.

Further reinforcing the power of humor, a study highlighted in PMC reveals that humor significantly lowers anxiety and depression levels. The researchers found that using humor as a coping strategy was linked to higher optimism and lower stress levels (Menéndez-Aller et al., 2020). Essentially, humor helps us navigate life's ups and downs with a lighter heart.

While humor is a valuable tool, it's essential to ensure it serves us positively. Sometimes humor can be used to deflect from deeper issues. Reflect on whether humor is being used constructively. If it feels like a shield from facing tough emotions, consider balancing laughter with moments of introspection.

Finally, embracing humor in daily life requires a bit of mindfulness and persistence. It's about creating a habit where laughter isn't reserved for special occasions but becomes woven into the fabric of our everyday experiences. Engaging with humor regularly helps build resilience and fosters a more optimistic outlook, even in the face of adversity.

# The Companionship and Emotional Support Provided by Pets

Pets have an extraordinary ability to offer unconditional love and companionship, acting as steadfast sources of comfort and emotional stability, especially during times of distress. Picture this: you've had a particularly rough day, where everything that could go wrong did go wrong. As you walk through the door, your pet greets you with boundless enthusiasm, their wagging tail or purring presence instantly lifting your spirits. This isn't just a warm, fuzzy feeling; it's a real, evidence-backed response. Pets can truly help soothe emotional turbulence. To harness this healing potential:

- Spend quality time each day with your pet, engaging in activities that both of you enjoy.

- Make it a habit to talk to your pet about your day, as verbalizing your thoughts can often lighten emotional burdens.

- Provide them with affection through petting or cuddling, which not only fosters your bond but also reduces stress.

Caring for a pet naturally encourages routines and physical activity, promoting a sense of purpose and structure that can significantly enhance daily life. Imagine the scenario: waking up every morning to the eager eyes of your dog waiting for their walk. This routine propels you out of bed and out into the world, providing a structured start to your day. Moreover, having a routine can be lifesaving when you're grappling with anxiety or depressive episodes.

In addition to routines and physical activity, interacting with pets has been shown to release oxytocin, commonly known as the "bonding hormone." This beneficial chemical fosters feelings of security, elevating mood and reducing anxiety levels without requiring any effort beyond simply being present with your pet. Whether it's stroking your cat while you binge-watch your favorite series or playing fetch with your dog in the park, these interactions are low-stress, high-reward activities.

Furthermore, the mere presence of a pet can significantly diminish feelings of isolation. In an increasingly digital and often lonely world, pets act as bridges to human connection. Owning a pet necessitates certain social interactions— whether it's chatting with other dog owners at the park or talking to the vet about your pet's health. These small engagements can collectively knit a fabric of social support around you, subtly improving your overall well-being.

Pets, albeit indirectly, play a vital role in expanding our social circles. They offer common ground and shared experiences that make initiating conversations easier and less daunting. For instance, dogs often initiate interactions with other dogs and their owners, creating opportunities for spontaneous human connections.

The emotional benefits of pets are profoundly impactful. Studies have shown that owning a pet is linked to lower risks of depression and better overall mental health (HelpGuide, n.d.-c). But how do we maximize these benefits? It comes down to integrating our pets fully into our lives:

- Engage in mutual activities that allow both of you to bond while enjoying nature, such as hiking or visiting pet-friendly beaches.

- Allow your pet to accompany you on errands or casual outings whenever feasible, thus infusing mundane tasks with more social facets.

- Incorporate training sessions that focus on fun tricks or commands, turning learning into an engaging experience for both parties.

Given these multifaceted benefits, it's evident that pets contribute enormously to our emotional landscape. Yet, it's crucial to balance these advantages with responsible pet ownership. Preparing for a pet's long-term commitment ensures that you and your furry friend thrive together. Here's how:

- Research thoroughly before choosing a pet to understand its needs and whether they align with your lifestyle.

- Budget for regular veterinary visits, nutritious food, grooming, and other essentials.

- Ensure your home environment is safe and comfortable for your pet, thereby fostering a space where they can thrive emotionally and physically.

To underscore the importance of this relationship, consider that pet owners frequently report lower blood pressure during stressful situations compared to non-owners (Kretzler et al., 2022). The physiological calming effects of having a pet nearby can transform how you navigate everyday stresses. Rather than viewing your pet merely as an animal, see them as an integral part of your support system.

## Bringing It All Together: Cultivating a Holistic Approach to Mental Well-Being

As we bring together the themes we've explored, it's clear that nature, creativity, humor, and companions like pets can profoundly influence our mental well-being. We've walked through forests and hiked up trails to understand how being in natural surroundings can lower stress hormones and uplift our spirits. Immersing ourselves in these environments doesn't just feel good; it's backed by research showing tangible benefits for our minds.

We've also dipped our toes into creative pursuits, from painting to writing, finding that they offer more than a simple hobby. They allow us to express and process emotions and even experience bursts of joy. Creativity becomes a sanctuary, a place where negative thoughts can transform into something beautiful and fulfilling. These activities can seamlessly fit into our daily routines, making a big difference with just a little time each day.

Laughter, too, emerged as an unexpected hero in dealing with anxiety. Humor helps lighten emotional loads, fosters connections with others, and releases those feel-good chemicals that shift our mood toward positivity. By integrating humor into our lives through shared jokes or funny videos, we can find relief and resilience, even when times are tough.

Then, there's the irreplaceable comfort of pets. Their unconditional love provides a steady anchor during stormy days. The routines and physical activities pets require help structure our lives, while their mere presence can foster feelings of safety and reduce loneliness. Pets offer companionship and a deeper connection that enhances our emotional stability.

You might wonder why these elements—nature, creativity, humor, pets—hold such power over our anxiety and overall mental health. It's because they help us reconnect with simpler joys and foster genuine moments of mindfulness and presence. They serve as reminders that small, everyday actions can lead to significant shifts in how we feel and cope.

In the grand scheme of things, embracing these tools may seem minor, yet their impact is profound. They offer sustainable ways to manage anxiety and enhance quality of life. So, take a moment today to step outside, create something new, laugh out loud, or simply enjoy the silent company of your furry friend. These choices pave the way to a more balanced and joyful existence, one mindful step at a time.

Let's cross over to the final chapter and look at long-term interventions that you can put in place to manage anxiety.

# Chapter 9:

# Sustaining Long-Term Anxiety

# Management

Navigating the journey to manage anxiety can feel like trying to climb a mountain without a map. Some days, the path is clear and easy to follow; other days, it's full of insurmountable obstacles. But just as every step counts when hiking up a steep trail, each moment of management progress adds up. It's reassuring to know that there's a way to chart this journey, making sure you don't get lost along the way.

Anxiety often manifests itself through various triggers and stressors that can feel overwhelming. For example, social gatherings may leave you feeling exhausted and apprehensive, while deadlines at work or school can seem impossible to meet. Recognizing these challenges is essential to managing them effectively over time. Achieving long-term emotional well-being is not about eliminating anxiety altogether—it's about learning how to deal with it constructively.

This involves setting realistic goals, tracking your progress, and adapting your strategies as needed. Think of it as building a toolkit that helps you cope better each day, slowly but surely reducing the impact anxiety has on your life. In this chapter, we'll delve into practical methods for sustaining long-term anxiety management.

You'll discover how setting and achieving realistic goals can boost your confidence and provide a sense of accomplishment. We'll discuss the significance of tracking your progress to stay motivated and recognize your improvements. Moreover, we'll explore the importance of being flexible and adjusting your goals based on changing circumstances or feedback. Celebrating small victories will also be emphasized as a way to reinforce positive behaviors. By adopting these practices, you're not just managing anxiety—you're building a foundation for lasting emotional well-being.

## Setting Realistic Goals and Tracking Progress in Anxiety Management

Setting achievable short-term and long-term goals can provide a sense of direction and accomplishment in managing anxiety. Imagine navigating your journey without a map; it's easy to feel lost. By setting realistic goals, we're essentially drawing out that map—giving ourselves signposts to look forward to and milestones to celebrate. To start, break down your overarching objectives into smaller, digestible chunks. If reducing daily anxiety is your goal, think of specific actions you can take each day.

Here's what you can do in order to achieve the goal:

- Identify the anxieties or triggers you wish to tackle.

- Choose simple, actionable steps to address each trigger. For instance, if social gatherings make you anxious, set a goal to attend a small event first.

- Define what success looks like for each step. For example, staying at the event for 30 minutes before leaving could be a measurable, attainable goal.

- Make sure these steps are time-bound, adding a deadline to keep you motivated and on track.

When we take these steps, our path becomes clearer and the sense of accomplishment from achieving short-term goals fuels us forward.

Regularly tracking progress toward these goals helps individuals stay motivated and recognize improvements in their anxiety management journey. It's fascinating how a small win, often overlooked in the hustle and bustle of daily life, can boost our morale immensely. Reflect on those moments when you've felt a surge of pride—perhaps after sticking to a morning meditation routine for a week or saying no to an overwhelming obligation without guilt.

Consider keeping a journal or using a progress-tracking app. Documenting your feelings, behaviors, and achievements creates a tangible record of progress.

By tracking progress, you not only stay aware of where you stand but also serve as a reminder of how far you've come, reinforcing the pursuit of better anxiety management (SLV Behavioral Health Group, n.d.).

Being flexible in adjusting goals based on changing circumstances or feedback can prevent feelings of failure and enhance resilience. Life is unpredictable, and rigidity can often lead to frustration when things don't go as planned. Flexibility allows you to pivot effortlessly, embracing change rather than resisting it.

For instance, don't hesitate to tweak a particular strategy without yielding the desired results. Maybe your initial goal of meditating for 20 minutes daily isn't feasible with your current schedule. Pivot and adjust the goal to 10 minutes. This adaptability doesn't mean you've failed—it signifies growth and understanding of your unique needs.

Flexibility transforms setbacks into valuable lessons, helping build resilience—a critical trait for anyone managing anxiety.

Celebrating small victories and milestones along the way can boost confidence and reinforce positive behaviors. Imagine running a marathon where there are no mile markers, no cheering crowds—only the start and finish lines. Exhausting, right? Celebrations serve as vital markers, reminding us that progress is being made even when the end goal seems far off.

Think of ways to reward yourself for sticking to your goals. Did you manage to complete a week of journaling? Treat yourself! Consider the following ways that you can celebrate your big and small victories:

- Set up a system of small rewards for achieving short-term goals. Maybe it's indulging in your favorite dessert or taking a relaxing bath.

- Share your victories with friends and family who understand your journey. Their support can amplify your satisfaction.

- Reflect on your successes and document them, making them a source of motivation during tougher days.

These celebrations aren't just about feeling good momentarily—they anchor your positive behaviors, creating a cycle of motivation and achievement.

Goal-setting and progress tracking are essential tools for sustaining long-term progress in anxiety management. When we take deliberate steps toward clear targets, track our advancements, remain adaptable, and acknowledge our achievements, we build a sustainable practice of self-care. This structured approach doesn't just reduce stress—it strengthens our overall emotional well-being.

Through this journey of setting and adjusting goals, tracking progress, and celebrating successes, we cultivate a habit of continuous self-improvement and resilience. Always remember, the path to managing anxiety is a marathon, not a sprint.

Embrace every small victory, learn from each setback, and always strive for progress, not perfection.

By integrating these practices into your life, you're not just managing anxiety; you're actively enhancing your emotional health, building a foundation for long-term well-being. Take it one step at a time, and soon, you'll find yourself coping and thriving in the face of life's challenges.

# Engaging in Ongoing Self-Care Practices and Seeking Continuous Growth

Prioritizing self-care activities such as exercise, eating healthy, and getting adequate rest can provide a strong foundation for overall emotional well-being and resilience. The science backs this up: regular physical activity has been proven to release endorphins—those feel-good hormones that boost your mood and alleviate stress (Raypole, 2022). A balanced diet provides the necessary nutrients your brain needs to function optimally, preventing those peaks and valleys in your energy levels that can exacerbate anxiety. Adequate rest is equally indispensable; without it, your body doesn't have the chance to reset, which can lead to heightened stress and irritability.

Seeking opportunities for personal growth through education, hobbies, or new experiences can open doors to a deeper sense of purpose and fulfillment beyond merely managing anxiety. Engaging in learning—whether picking up a new language, diving into online courses, or simply exploring a subject you're passionate about—stimulates the mind and offers refreshing perspectives on life. Hobbies are similarly beneficial, providing an outlet to express creativity and derive satisfaction from small achievements. Whether it's painting, gardening, or playing a musical instrument, these activities can offer a much-needed break from the daily grind and help rejuvenate your spirit.

Personal growth need not be limited to structured or formal activities. Sometimes, it's about embracing spontaneity—trying out a new café, traveling to an unfamiliar locale, or even taking a different route home. These little changes can disrupt the monotony and bring unexpected joy and discovery into your life.

Engaging in regular self-reflection and introspection allows you to identify triggers, patterns, and areas for improvement in management. Self-reflection serves as a mirror that you hold up to your inner world, helping you understand the root causes of your stress and anxiety. It's crucial to reserve time for this practice regularly—perhaps weekly or monthly—to take stock of your emotional landscape.

Practicing self-compassion and forgiveness toward oneself is a cornerstone for maintaining a positive relationship with personal growth and self-care. We often reserve our harshest judgments for ourselves, setting unrealistically high expectations and then chastising ourselves when we fall short. Shifting this pattern involves treating yourself with the same kindness and understanding you would extend to a friend.

Research reveals that medical students who consistently self-care report less stress and a higher quality of life (Ayala et al., 2018). Extending this concept universally underscores the critical importance of ongoing self-care routines—not just as a remedy during stressful periods but as a preventative measure to maintain emotional equilibrium. Similarly, another study highlights how engaging in self-care can significantly mitigate the adverse effects of perceived stress, thereby protecting one's psychological well-being (Luis et al., 2021).

Continuous self-care and a growth mindset are vital components of sustaining long-term anxiety management. However, remember that balance is key. It's a journey, not a destination, and there will always be room for improvement and adaptation as life presents new challenges.

In chapters 7 and 8, we looked at several lifestyle changes that play a crucial role in managing anxiety levels. These changes, though simple, form a foundation for effective self-care. Diet, exercise, sleep, and digital habits significantly impact one's mental health, highlighting the importance of conscious choices in everyday life. Incorporating calming practices such as mindfulness, exposure to nature, creative activities, humor, and interactions with pets can further alleviate anxiety. Natural environments, creative outlets, humor, and human connections serve as powerful tools in reducing stress and promoting emotional well-being. Integrating these holistic approaches into daily routines, individuals can achieve a more balanced and peaceful state of mind, fostering resilience and a greater sense of control over their anxiety.

# Developing a Relapse Prevention Plan for Potential Setbacks

When you've been working hard to manage anxiety, the thought of a relapse can be daunting. But remember, understanding and preparing for potential setbacks is crucial in maintaining long-term emotional well-being. Developing a relapse prevention plan isn't just about avoiding those tough moments—it's about empowering yourself with tools and strategies to stay on track.

## *Identify Early Warning Signs or Triggers*

Knowing what triggers your anxiety is the first step toward intervening proactively. Everyone has unique triggers, whether they are specific situations, thoughts, or even physical sensations. For example, your anxiety might spike when you're in crowded places or when deadlines loom.

Here is what you can do to identify early warning signs:

- **Reflect on Past Experiences:** Think about the times your anxiety was at its worst. What were the common factors? Were there any patterns in your environment or behavior?

- **Monitor Your Emotions:** Keep a journal to note down daily feelings and events. Over time, this can reveal trends that indicate your triggers.

- **Seek Feedback:** Sometimes, others see our warning signs before we do. Ask trusted friends or family members if they've noticed certain behaviors when you're feeling anxious.

- **Use Technology:** There are apps designed to help track mood swings and anxiety levels, providing insights into potential triggers.

By recognizing these early signs, you can take action before anxiety becomes overwhelming.

### *Create a Personalized Coping Strategy or Crisis Plan*

Having a personalized coping strategy gives you a roadmap to navigate severe anxiety episodes. This sense of preparedness can provide significant peace of mind.

Here's how you can create your own plan:

- **Define Your Steps:** Outline specific actions you will take when you notice early warning signs. It could be taking a break, going for a walk, or practicing deep breathing exercises.

- **Identify Support Contacts:** List the people you can reach out to when you're struggling. Ensure they're aware they are part of your support plan.

- **Prepare Emergency Tools:** This might include soothing music playlists, stress balls, or calming scents like lavender. Having these readily available can make a big difference during high-stress moments.

- **Practice Coping Techniques:** Incorporate techniques such as mindfulness, progressive muscle relaxation, or guided imagery into your daily routine. These practices become more effective the more you use them.

Creating this plan isn't just about managing anxiety when it happens; it's also about reducing its overall impact on your life.

## *Seek Support From Mental Health Professionals or Support Groups*

You don't have to face anxiety alone. Professional help and support groups can offer resources and guidance that enhance your relapse prevention efforts.

To seek support effectively:

- **Consult Professionals:** A therapist or counselor can provide tailored strategies and tools for managing anxiety. Cognitive-behavioral therapy (CBT), for instance, has been shown to be particularly effective (Zgierska, 2014).

- **Join Support Groups:** Whether online or in-person, connecting with others who understand your experiences can provide emotional support and practical advice. Look into organizations like the Anxiety and Depression Association of America (ADAA) for groups that fit your needs.

- **Leverage Community Resources:** Many communities offer free or low-cost mental health resources. Libraries, community centers, and healthcare providers can often point you in the right direction.

- **Educate Yourself:** Reading books, attending workshops, or participating in webinars about anxiety can increase your understanding and provide new techniques for your management plan.

Regularly engaging with professional and peer support networks ensures you have a robust safety net to catch you should you start to slip.

## Practice Self-Awareness and Self-Regulation Techniques

Self-awareness and self-regulation are powerful skills in preventing anxiety setbacks. You can better manage your reactions by being attuned to your thoughts and emotions.

To cultivate these skills:

- **Mindfulness Meditation:** Practicing mindfulness helps you stay present and reduces rumination on past or future worries. Even a few minutes each day can improve your ability to manage anxiety (Krijnen-de Bruin et al., 2022).

- **Deep Breathing Exercises:** Learning to control your breath can calm your nervous system quickly. Techniques like 4-7-8 breathing (inhale for 4 seconds, hold for 7, exhale for 8) can be particularly helpful.

- **Regular Self-Check-ins:** Set aside time daily to reflect on your internal state. Ask yourself how you're feeling and why. This practice can prevent small stressors from building up unnoticed.

- **Healthy Habits:** Regular exercise, balanced nutrition, and adequate sleep are foundational to emotional well-being. Physical health significantly impacts mental health, making these habits non-negotiable.

- **Stress Management Techniques:** Identify activities that reduce your stress, such as hobbies, spending time in nature, or engaging in creative pursuits. Make time for these regularly.

Having a relapse prevention plan enhances your resilience and readiness to manage potential setbacks in anxiety management. By understanding your triggers, creating a coping strategy, seeking support, and practicing self-awareness, you build a comprehensive toolkit that empowers you to maintain progress and continue improving your anxiety management skills.

Incorporating these steps into your daily life isn't just about avoiding anxiety—it's about enhancing your overall emotional well-being and leading a more balanced, fulfilling life. Remember, the aim is progress, not perfection. Every effort you make counts toward sustaining your long-term emotional health.

# Creating a Supportive Environment and Nurturing a Positive Mindset for Sustained Anxiety Management

Surrounding oneself with a supportive network of friends, family, or mental health professionals can offer encouragement and validation in the anxiety management journey. Imagine your life as a group activity, where each person in your circle plays an essential role in creating a safe space for you to thrive. By connecting deeply with those who uplift and encourage you, you build a safety net that cushions you during stressful times.

Friends can be your cheerleaders when the going gets tough, providing both perspective and emotional reinforcement. Family can be your grounding force, often offering unconditional love and understanding. And let's not forget mental health professionals, who bring clinical wisdom and objective guidance to the table. According to research by LCMC Health (2023), our social environment significantly impacts our mental health. A supportive network reduces feelings of isolation and fosters a sense of belonging, which is vital for sustained anxiety management.

Switching gears, let's talk about cultivating an optimistic outlook through gratitude practices, affirmations, or positive self-talk. Studies have shown that these practices can shift focus toward resilience and growth. Here is what you can do in order to achieve this:

- Start your day with gratitude. List three things you're thankful for before getting out of bed.

- Use affirmations throughout the day. Simple statements like "I am capable" or "I choose calm" can redirect your thoughts positively.

- Engage in positive self-talk. When you catch yourself thinking negatively, challenge those thoughts and replace them with constructive ones.

- End your day by reflecting on what went well. This reinforces a mindset of appreciation and progress.

When we practice gratitude and positive self-talk, we are essentially rewiring our brains to notice and prioritize the good in our lives. This simple but powerful shift helps us develop resilience, enabling us to bounce back more quickly from setbacks (National Institutes of Health (NIH), 2017).

Establishing boundaries with toxic relationships or environments that trigger anxiety is another critical step. Boundaries act as personal protective barriers, ensuring that our well-being isn't compromised by external negativity. The process of setting boundaries starts by identifying who or what drains your energy. Once identified, here is what you can do:

- Communicate your limits. Let others know what behaviors are unacceptable to you.

- Limit interactions with toxic individuals or environments. If possible, remove yourself from situations that cause distress.

- Practice saying no without guilt. Your mental health should always come first.

- Reinforce your boundaries consistently. Over time, people will learn to respect them.

Creating a safe and nurturing space begins with safeguarding our emotional territory. When we set clear boundaries, we give ourselves permission to protect our peace and prioritize our well-being. Engaging in acts of kindness, community involvement, or social connections can foster a sense of belonging and purpose, fueling sustained anxiety management. Simple acts of kindness—helping a neighbor or volunteering at a local shelter—do wonders for your mental health. They create a ripple effect, spreading positivity both inwardly and outwardly. Community involvement allows you to connect with others who share similar values and interests, further reinforcing your support network. Social connections, whether through joining a club or participating in group activities, provide opportunities to build meaningful relationships and shared experiences.

The key takeaway here is that creating a supportive and positive environment is essential for maintaining long-term emotional well-being and resilience in anxiety management. Think of it like tending to a garden; it requires consistent effort, attention, and care. By surrounding yourself with supportive people, cultivating a positive mindset, establishing boundaries, and engaging with your community, you lay the groundwork for a healthier, more resilient you.

While taking proactive steps to manage anxiety may feel daunting, think of it as an ongoing journey rather than a destination. Every small action counts, contributing to your overall emotional health. Remember, it's okay to seek help and lean on your support system. You're not alone in this journey, and with continued effort, you've got everything you need to thrive.

## Consolidating Long-Term Success in Anxiety Management

In wrapping up our exploration of maintaining progress and continuously improving anxiety management skills, let's revisit the core tenets we've discussed. We've delved into the importance of setting realistic goals and tracking progress, emphasizing how breaking down larger objectives into smaller, achievable steps can provide direction and a sense of accomplishment. Regularly reflecting on these small victories serves as motivation and evidence of personal growth over time.

Adapting to changing circumstances by staying flexible with your goals ensures that you remain resilient even when life throws unexpected challenges your way. Flexibility isn't a sign of failure; rather, it's a testament to your understanding and respect for your personal needs and capacities. This adaptability empowers you to tweak your strategies for managing anxiety as necessary, allowing for a more personalized approach to well-being.

The journey also involves celebrating your milestones. These celebrations act as motivational markers, reinforcing positive behavior and providing emotional boosts. Feeling good about reaching these mini-goals creates a cycle of continued effort and success, ensuring long-term adherence to anxiety management practices.

By engaging in ongoing self-care practices like regular exercise, balanced nutrition, and ample rest, you lay a solid foundation for emotional health. Personal growth through hobbies, education, or new experiences further enriches your life, offering fulfillment beyond merely coping with anxiety. Self-reflection helps maintain this balance by providing insights into triggers and patterns, enabling you to make informed adjustments to your strategies.

We also touched upon the significance of nurturing a positive mindset through gratitude, affirmations, and positive self-talk. These practices help reshape your perspective, making it easier to focus on growth and resilience. Setting boundaries protects your mental space from toxic influences, ensuring you're surrounded by supportive, encouraging individuals.

As you continue this journey, keep in mind that the ultimate goal is continuous growth, not perfection. Each step forward, no matter how small, contributes to a more balanced and fulfilling life. By integrating these practices into your daily routine, you're not just addressing anxiety; you're actively cultivating a healthier, more resilient version of yourself.

The road may have its ups and downs, but with dedication and self-compassion, you'll find yourself not just managing but thriving amidst life's challenges. Take one step at a time, always strive for progress, and never underestimate the power of small victories in shaping a calmer, more centered you.

We will now proceed to the conclusion and take stock of everything we have learned on this journey of coping with anxiety.

# Conclusion

Imagine building a house. Each brick laid represents an anxiety management technique, and each tool used—be it CBT, meditation, or maintaining healthy relationships—supports construction. Over time, your house becomes a sturdy sanctuary against the storms of anxiety. It's not just about using one method but integrating multiple approaches harmoniously to create a resilient structure.

Moreover, it's essential to maintain a balanced perspective. Life is not devoid of stress, but mastering anxiety management equips you better to handle life's inevitable ups and downs. Think of these techniques as physical exercise for your mind—just as consistent workouts build muscle strength, regularly practicing these strategies strengthens your emotional resilience and mental agility.

It's also vital to acknowledge that seeking professional help is a sign of strength, not weakness. Therapists and counselors are trained to guide you through these processes, offering tailored advice and support. Sometimes, an external viewpoint can illuminate aspects of anxiety you hadn't considered, providing valuable insights and facilitating breakthroughs in your journey toward better mental health.

While we may be tempted to view anxiety solely as a mental burden, let's also recognize its potential to catalyze personal growth. Confronting and managing anxiety forces us to develop skills that often spill over into other areas of our lives, enhancing our overall quality of life. When you learn to navigate your emotions, you also become more adept at handling other forms of stress, improving your ability to juggle life's myriad demands.

The journey to long-term anxiety management is deeply personal yet universally impactful, underscored by the lifestyle changes you choose to embrace. As you navigate your path, remember that your diet, exercise, sleep, and digital habits are pivotal in shaping your mental health. Embracing natural environments, engaging in creative activities, sharing laughter, and fostering human connections are temporary fixes and essential tools for sustaining mental well-being. Through these holistic approaches, you can cultivate a more balanced and peaceful state of mind, empowering yourself to lead a life marked by resilience and serenity. Remember, you have the power to shape your journey, and with these strategies, long-term relief is not just a possibility but a promise.

## Real-Life Success and Encouragement

One particularly inspiring story involves a young woman named Sophie. Sophie was in her early twenties, just starting out in her career, juggling work, family, and personal life demands. She often felt overwhelmed and anxious, struggling to keep up with the pace and expectations around her. At her worst, she experienced panic attacks that left her feeling isolated and powerless.

Sophie knew she needed to make a change. She started by identifying her triggers—situations that consistently induced stress. This step is crucial because understanding what sparks your anxiety allows you to address it more effectively. Sophie realized that certain work-related tasks and social gatherings were her main triggers. With this awareness, she began employing cognitive-behavioral techniques to reframe her negative thoughts. When she felt anxious about a presentation at work, for instance, she would challenge those fears by asking herself rational questions: "What's the worst that could happen?" or "How likely is it that my fear will come true?"

Visualization techniques also played a significant role in Sophie's journey. Before stepping into anxiety-inducing situations, she would spend a few quiet moments visualizing a positive outcome. She pictured herself delivering an engaging presentation or enjoying a social event. This practice didn't eliminate her anxiety entirely, but it equipped her with a sense of calm and control, enabling her to face challenges more confidently.

Emotional resilience became another cornerstone of Sophie's strategy. Building resilience means cultivating the ability to bounce back from stressful episodes. Sophie did this by maintaining healthy relationships. Supportive friends and family provided a buffer against anxiety, offering advice, empathy, or simply a listening ear. By leaning on her support network, she reinforced her emotional stability, making it easier to cope during tough times.

Sophie's journey also involved incorporating meditation, self-reflection, and gratitude practices into her daily routine. Each morning, she spent ten minutes meditating, focusing on her breath, and grounding herself in the present moment. This simple act helped her start her day with a clear and calm mind. Reflecting on her experiences allowed Sophie to gain insights into her emotional patterns, which furthered her understanding of her anxiety. Practicing gratitude shifted her focus from stressors to the positives in her life, fostering a more optimistic outlook.

If you're struggling with anxiety, consider taking a leaf out of Sophie's book:

- Identify your triggers. Pay attention to the situations or activities that consistently cause stress.

- Challenge negative thoughts using cognitive-behavioral techniques. Ask yourself rational questions to break the cycle of fear.

- Use visualization techniques. Picture positive outcomes before facing anxiety-inducing situations.

- Build emotional resilience by maintaining healthy relationships. Lean on your support network for advice and comfort.

- Incorporate meditation, self-reflection, and gratitude practices into your daily routine to promote emotional well-being.

Sophie's story is a testament to the power of consistent effort and the right strategies for managing anxiety. Remember, overcoming anxiety is not a linear process; there will be ups and downs. However, with dedication and the right tools, it's possible to regain control over your life.

Now, I'm inviting you to take action. Practice the techniques we've discussed throughout this book regularly. Remember, consistency is key. If you find yourself struggling despite your best efforts, don't hesitate to seek professional help.

Therapists and counselors can offer additional support and tailored strategies to manage your mental health.

Sharing your experiences can also be incredibly empowering for yourself and others. By talking about our struggles and triumphs, we can foster a supportive community where no one feels alone in their journey. Reach out, share your story, and listen to others. Through our collective experiences, we can build a stronger, more resilient community.

In closing, mastering anxiety management techniques can significantly enhance your quality of life. Armed with the right tools and practices, you're surviving and thriving. You'll find yourself navigating life's challenges with greater ease and confidence, paving the way for a more fulfilling existence.

So go ahead. Take the first step today. Identify your triggers, practice mindfulness, lean on your loved ones, and always remember that seeking help is a sign of strength, not weakness. Let's walk this path together, supporting each other along the way. We've got this.

# References

acburton. (2024, March 21). *Nurturing a growth mindset to overcome writing challenges and develop confidence in college level writing.* Writing Center. https://writingcenter.uci.edu/2024/03/21/nurturing-a-growth-mindset-to-overcome-writing-challenges-and-develop-confidence-in-college-level-writing/

Alborzkouh, P., Nabati, M., Zainali, M., Abed, Y., & Shahgholy Ghahfarokhi, F. (2015). A review of the effectiveness of stress management. *Journal of Medicine and Life, 8*(4), 39. https://pubmed.ncbi.nlm.nih.gov/28316704/

*Any anxiety disorder.* (n.d.). National Institute of Mental Health. https://www.nimh.nih.gov/health/statistics/any-anxiety-disorder

*Anxiety disorders.* (n.d.). National Institute of Mental Health. https://www.nimh.nih.gov/health/topics/anxiety-disorders

*Anxiety disorders - facts & statistics.* (2022, October 28). Anxiety and Depression Association of America. https://adaa.org/understanding-anxiety/facts-statistics

Ayala, E. E., Winseman, J. S., Johnsen, R. D., & Mason, H. R. C. (2018). U.S. medical students who engage in self-care report less stress and higher quality of life. *BMC Medical Education*, *18*(10), 1-8. https://doi.org/10.1186/s12909-018-1296-x

Bandelow, B., & Michaelis, S. (2022, April 1). *Epidemiology of anxiety disorders in the 21st century. Dialogues in Clinical Neuroscience*, *17*(3), 327. https://doi.org/10.31887/DCNS.2015.17.3/bbandelow

Bailey, J., & Rehman, S. (2022, March 4). *Don't underestimate the power of self-reflection*. Harvard Business Review. https://hbr.org/2022/03/dont-underestimate-the-power-of-self-reflection

Black, P., Henderson-Smith, L., & Flinspach, S. (2021, September 21). *Trauma-informed, resilience-oriented schools toolkit*. National Center for School Safety. https://www.nc2s.org/resource/trauma-informed-resilience-oriented-schools-toolkit/

Bleile, C. (n.d.). *Supporting individuals with anxiety: Effective strategies and communication tips*. MercyOne. https://www.mercyone.org/health-and-wellness/health-answers/behavioral-health/supporting-individuals-with-anxiety-effective-strategies-and-communication-tips

Brown, J., & Wong, J.. (2017, June 6). How gratitude changes you and your brain. *Greater Good Magazine*.

https://greatergood.berkeley.edu/article/item/how_g
ratitude_changes_you_and_your_brain

Can Fam Physician. (2011, November). Part 12. Systematic
desensitization. *Canadian Family Physician*, *57*(11), 1299.
https://www.ncbi.nlm.nih.gov/pmc/articles/PMC32
15612/

Caporuscip, P. (2020, April 1). *What is relationship anxiety?*
MedicalNewsToday.
http://skinandwound.org/relationship-anxiety.html

Chand, S. P., & Marwaha, R. (2023). *Anxiety.* National
Library of Medicine.
https://www.ncbi.nlm.nih.gov/books/NBK470361/

*Communication and boundaries.* (n.d.). Center for Mindful
Therapy. https://mindfulcenter.org/communication-
and-boundaries/

Corliss, J. (2022, February 2). *Six relaxation techniques to reduce
stress.* Harvard Health.
https://www.health.harvard.edu/mind-and-
mood/six-relaxation-techniques-to-reduce-stress

*Could negative thinking patterns be bringing you down? Recognizing
cognitive distortions is the first step to overcoming them.* (n.d.).
CHC.
https://www.chconline.org/resourcelibrary/negative-
thinking-patterns-and-how-to-overcome-them/

Crego, A., Yela, J. R., Riesco-Matías, P., Gómez-Martínez,
M.-Á., Vicente-Arruebarrena, A., et al. (2022, July 22).

The benefits of self-compassion in mental health professionals: A systematic review of empirical research. *Psychology Research and Behavior Management, 15*, 2599. https://doi.org/10.2147/PRBM.S359382

Curtiss, J. E., Levine, D. S., Ander, I., & Baker, A. W. (2021, June 17). Cognitive-behavioral treatments for anxiety and stress-related disorders. *Focus, 19*(2), 184. https://doi.org/10.1176/appi.focus.20200045

Davis, D. & Hayes, J. (2012). *What are the benefits of mindfulness?* American Psychological Association. https://www.apa.org/monitor/2012/07-08/ce-corner

*8 soothing techniques to help relieve anxiety.* (2020, April 24). University Hospitals. https://www.uhhospitals.org/blog/articles/2020/04/8-soothing-techniques-to-help-relieve-anxiety

*Emotional wellness toolkit.* (n.d.). National Institutes of Health. https://www.nih.gov/health-information/emotional-wellness-toolkit

*Exposure therapy.* (n.d.). Cleveland Clinic. https://my.clevelandclinic.org/health/treatments/25067-exposure-therapy

Felman, A. (2023, May 19). *What causes anxiety?* Medical News Today. http://skinandwound.org/323456.html

Fleming, L. (n.d.). *Using humor as a healthy coping mechanism.* Jed Foundation.

https://jedfoundation.org/resource/using-humor-as-a-healthy-coping-mechanism/

*Getting enough sleep.* (2023, August 4). OASH. https://health.gov/myhealthfinder/healthy-living/mental-health-and-relationships/get-enough-sleep

Global Counseling Solutions, PLLC. (2022, October 10). *How Anxiety Affects Relationships. Global counseling solutions.* https://globalcounselingsolutions.org/how-anxiety-affects-relationships/

Gómez, A. F., & Hofmann, S. G. (2017). Mindfulness-based interventions for anxiety and depression. *The Psychiatric Clinics of North America, 40*(4), 739. https://doi.org/10.1016/j.psc.2017.08.008

Godron, R. (2023, May 16). *Overcoming test anxiety: 11 strategies to help reduce your stress.* American Public University. https://www.apu.apus.edu/area-of-study/electrical-engineering/resources/overcoming-test-anxiety/

*Grounding techniques for anxiety.* (n.d.). Meridian University. https://meridianuniversity.edu/content/grounding-techniques-for-anxiety

Hamblen, J. & Mueser, K. (2021). *Treatment for postdisaster distress.* American Psychological Association. https://www.apa.org/pubs/books/treatment-for-postdisaster-distress

Hartley, C. A., & Phelps, E. A. (2012). Anxiety and decision-making. *Biological Psychiatry, 72*(2), 10.1016/j.biopsych.2011.12.027. https://doi.org/10.1016/j.biopsych.2011.12.027

Hengen, K. M., & Alpers, G. W. (2021, February 21). Stress makes the difference: Social stress and social anxiety in decision-making under uncertainty. *Frontiers in Psychology, 12*(Article 578293). https://doi.org/10.3389/fpsyg.2021.578293

Herbert, M. (2024, March 27). *Empathic listening: definition, examples, and skills.* TopResume. https://www.topresume.com/career-advice/empathic-listening-definition-examples-and-skills

Hernandez, S. (2024). Fostering resilience: tools for overcoming mental health challenges. *Painted Brain.* https://paintedbrain.org/painted-brain-media/blogs/mental-health/fostering-resilience-tools-for-overcoming-mental-health-challenges

Hofmann, S. G., & Gómez, A. F. (2017). Mindfulness-based interventions for anxiety and depression. *The Psychiatric Clinics of North America, 40*(4), 739. https://doi.org/10.1016/j.psc.2017.08.008

Hood, J. (2020, February 3). *The benefits and importance of a support system.* Highland Springs Clinic. https://highlandspringsclinic.org/the-benefits-and-importance-of-a-support-system/

*How setting goals can positively impact our mental health.* (n.d.). Centerstone. https://centerstone.org/our-resources/health-wellness/how-setting-goals-can-positively-impact-our-mental-health/

Huang, X., Zhang, Y., Wu, X., Jiang, Y., Cai, H., Deng, Y., Luo, Y., Zhao, L., Liu, Q., Luo, S., Wang, Y., Zhao, L., Jiang, M., & Wu, Y. (2023). A cross-sectional study: family communication, anxiety, and depression in adolescents: the mediating role of family violence and problematic internet use. *BMC Public Health*, 23(10). https://doi.org/10.1186/s12889-023-16637-0

Hutchison, M. (2021, January 12). Accessible self-soothing coping strategies. *Johns Hopkins University.* https://wellbeing.jhu.edu/blog/2021/01/12/accessible-self-soothing-coping-strategies/

*The importance of setting boundaries and saying no.* (n.d.). PAPYRUS. https://www.papyrus-uk.org/setting-boundaries/

International Journal of Nursing Studies. (2019). A self-compassion intervention to improve mental well-being among South African healthcare providers during COVID-19: A randomized controlled trial. *International Journal of Nursing Studies*, 103402. https://awspntest.apa.org/doi/10.1016/j.ijnurstu.2019.103402

Jimenez, M.P., DeVille, N.V., Elliott, E.G., Schiff, J.E., Wilt, G.E., Hart, J.E., & James, P. (2021). Associations between Nature Exposure and Health: A Review of the Evidence. *International Journal of Environmental Research and Public Health*, *18*(9), 4790. https://doi.org/10.3390/ijerph18094790.

Khan, S. (2023, March 31). *My battle with anxiety*. American Psychiatric Association of America. https://adaa.org/living-with-anxiety/personal-stories/my-battle-anxiety

Klein, R. J., Jacobson, N. C., & Robinson, M. D. (2023). A psychological flexibility perspective on well-being: Emotional reactivity, adaptive choices, and daily experiences. *Emotion*. 23(4), 911-924. https://doi.org/10.1037/emo0001159

Kretzler, B., König, H.-H., & Hajek, A. (2022). Pet ownership, loneliness, and social isolation: a systematic review. *Social Psychiatry and Psychiatric Epidemiology*, 57(10), 1935. https://doi.org/10.1007/s00127-022-02332-9

Krijnen-de Bruin, E., Scholten, W., Muntingh, A., Maarsingh, O., van Meijel, B., van Straten, A., & Batelaan, N. (2022, August 12). *Psychological interventions to prevent relapse in anxiety and depression: A systematic review and meta-analysis*. *PLoS ONE*, *17*(8), 10.1371/journal.pone.0272200. https://doi.org/10.1371/journal.pone.0272200

LCMC Health. (2023, May 30). *Creating a calm and supportive environment for your mental health*.

https://www.lcmchealth.org/university-medical-center-new-orleans/blog/2023/may/creating-a-calm-and-supportive-environment-for-y/

Luis, E., Bermejo-Martins, E., Martinez, M., Sarrionandia, A., Cortes, C., Oliveros, E. Y., Garces, M. S., Oron, J. V., & Fernández-Berrocal, P. (2021). Relationship between self-care activities, stress and well-being during COVID-19 lockdown: a cross-cultural mediation model. *BMJ Open, 12*(11). https://doi.org/10.1136/bmjopen-2020-048469

*Manage stress: Strengthen your support network.* (2022, October 21). American Psychological Association. https://www.apa.org/topics/stress/manage-social-support

Mayo Clinic Staff. (2022). *Mindfulness exercises.* Mayo Clinic. https://www.mayoclinic.org/healthy-lifestyle/consumer-health/in-depth/mindfulness-exercises/art-20046356.

Mayo Clinic Staff. (2023). *Meditation: A simple, fast way to reduce stress. Mayo Clinic.* https://www.mayoclinic.org/tests-procedures/meditation/in-depth/meditation/art-20045858

Mayo Clinic Staff. (2024). *Relaxation techniques: Try these steps to lower stress.* Mayo Clinic. https://www.mayoclinic.org/healthy-lifestyle/stress-management/in-depth/relaxation-technique/art-20045368

Mendlowicz, M. V., & Stein, M. B. (2000). *Quality of life in individuals with anxiety disorders. American Journal of Psychiatry, 157*(5), 669. https://doi.org/10.1176/appi.ajp.157.5.669

Menéndez-Aller, Á., Postigo, Á., Montes-Álvarez, P., González-Primo, F. J., & García-Cueto, E. (2020). Humor as a protective factor against anxiety and depression. *International Journal of Clinical and Health Psychology, 20*(1), 38. https://doi.org/10.1016/j.ijchp.2019.12.002

*The mental health benefits of creativity.* (n.d.). Diversus Health. https://diversushealth.org/mental-health-blog/the-mental-health-benefits-of-creativity/

Mental Health First Aid. (2020, August 6). *The importance of having a support system.* Mental Health First Aid. https://www.mentalhealthfirstaid.org/2020/08/the-importance-of-having-a-support-system/

Mindful Staff. (n.d.). Meditation for anxiety. *Mindful.* https://www.mindful.org/mindfulness-meditation-anxiety/

Modern Recovery Editorial Team. (2023, July 25). *Cognitive restructuring: definition, benefits & techniques.* Modern Recovery. https://modernrecoveryservices.com/wellness/coping/skills/cognitive/cognitive-restructuring/

Naidoo, U. (2020, October 27). Eating well to help manage anxiety: Your questions answered. *Harvard Health Blog.* https://www.health.harvard.edu/blog/eating-well-to-help-manage-anxiety-your-questions-answered-2018031413460

Nakshine, V. S., Thute, P., Khatib, M. N., & Sarkar, B. (2022). Increased screen time as a cause of declining physical, psychological health, and sleep patterns: A literary review. *Cureus, 14*(10). https://doi.org/10.7759/cureus.30051

Ng, B. (2018). The neuroscience of growth mindset and intrinsic motivation. *Brain Sciences, 8*(2), 20. https://doi.org/10.3390/brainsci8020020

Norelli, S. K., Long, A., & Krepps, J. M. (2023, August 4). Relaxation techniques. National Library of Medicine. https://pubmed.ncbi.nlm.nih.gov/30020610/

Pratt, M. (2022, February 17). *The science of gratitude. Mindful.* https://www.mindful.org/the-science-of-gratitude/

Raypole, C. (2022, July 26). *How to hack your hormones for a better mood.* Healthline. https://www.healthline.com/health/happy-hormone

Reid, S.. (2024, February 5). *Setting healthy boundaries in relationships.* HelpGuide.org. https://www.helpguide.org/articles/relationships-communication/setting-healthy-boundaries-in-relationships.htm

Robberegt, S. J., Brouwer, M. E., Kooiman, B. E. A. M., Stikkelbroek, Y. A. J., Nauta, M. H., & Bockting, C. L. H. (2023). Meta-analysis: relapse prevention strategies for depression and anxiety in remitted adolescents and young adults. *Journal of the American Academy of Child and Adolescent Psychiatry*, 62(3), 1-10. https://doi.org/10.1016/j.jaac.2022.04.014

Robinson, & L., Segal. (2024, February 5). *The health and mood-boosting benefits of pets.* HelpGuide.org. https://www.helpguide.org/articles/mental-health/mood-boosting-power-of-dogs.htm

Robinson, L., Segal, & J., Smith, M. (2024, February 5). *Relaxation techniques for stress relief.* HelpGuide.org. https://www.helpguide.org/articles/stress/relaxation-techniques-for-stress-relief.htm

Robinson, O. J., Vytal, K., Cornwell, B. R., & Grillon, C. (2013). The impact of anxiety upon cognition: perspectives from human threat of shock studies. *Frontiers in Human Neuroscience*, 7(10), 203. https://doi.org/10.3389/fnhum.2013.00203

Ross, S. (2020, March 27). *Healthy coping skills and self-soothing activities.* NAMI Dane County. https://www.namidanecounty.org/blog/2020/3/27/healthy-coping-skills-and-self-soothing-activities

Rhohovit, J. (n.d.). *Guide to goal setting and tracking.* Center for Practice Transformation.

https://practicetransformation.umn.edu/practice-tools/guide-to-goal-setting-and-tracking/

Sawchuk, C. (2017, May 24). *Coping with anxiety: Can diet make a difference?* Mayo Clinic. https://www.mayoclinic.org/diseases-conditions/generalized-anxiety-disorder/expert-answers/coping-with-anxiety/faq-20057987

Scott, A. J., Webb, T. L., Martyn-St James, M., Rowse, G., & Weich, S. (2021). Improving sleep quality leads to better mental health: A meta-analysis of randomised controlled trials. *Sleep Medicine Reviews*, 60, 10.1016/j.smrv.2021.101556. https://doi.org/10.1016/j.smrv.2021.101556

*Self-acceptance and self-compassion.* (n.d.). Anderson University. https://anderson.edu/student-life/counseling/self-acceptance-and-self-compassion/

Shuper Engelhard, E., Pitluk, M., & Elboim-Gabyzon, M. (2021). Grounding the connection between psyche and soma: Creating a reliable observation tool for grounding assessment in an adult population. *Frontiers in Psychology*, *12*, 10.3389/fpsyg.2021.621958. https://doi.org/10.3389/fpsyg.2021.621958

SLV Behavioral Health Group. (n.d.). *New year, new beginnings: setting realistic and achievable mental health goals.* https://www.slvbhg.org/post/new-year-new-beginnings-setting-realistic-and-achievable-mental-health-goals

Smith, S. (2018, April 10). *5-4-3-2-1 coping technique for anxiety*. Behavioral Health Partners. https://www.urmc.rochester.edu/behavioral-health-partners/bhp-blog/april-2018/5-4-3-2-1-coping-technique-for-anxiety.aspx

*Stress management: meditation, relaxation, health benefits*. (n.d.). Cleveland Clinic. https://my.clevelandclinic.org/health/treatments/6409-stress-management-and-emotional-health

Suni, E, & Dimitriu, A. (2024, March 26). *Mental health and sleep*. Sleep Foundation. https://www.sleepfoundation.org/mental-health

Sutton, A. (2016). Measuring the effects of self-awareness: construction of the self-awareness outcomes questionnaire. *Europe's Journal of Psychology*, 12(4), 645. https://doi.org/10.5964/ejop.v12i4.1178

Talago, L. (2023, June 2). *Self-compassion: a good rx guide to being kind to yourself*. GoodRx. https://www.goodrx.com/health-topic/mental-health/self-compassion-definition-exercises

Tiret, H. (2023, February 13). *Active listening and empathy for human connection*. Healthy Relationships. https://www.canr.msu.edu/news/active-listening-and-empathy-for-human-connection

Topic Expert Contributor. (2014). Anxiety and relationships: seven tips to improve communication. *GoodTherapy*.

https://www.goodtherapy.org/blog/anxiety-relationships-seven-tips-to-improve-communication-0210145/

Toussaint, L., Nguyen, Q. A., Roettger, C., Dixon, K., Offenbacher, M., Khols, N., Hirsch, J., & Sirois, F. (2021, July 3). Effectiveness of progressive muscle relaxation, deep breathing, and guided imagery in promoting psychological and physiological states of relaxation. *Wiley.* 2021, 5924040. https://doi.org/10.1155/2021/5924040

Uclahealth. (2023, May 22). *Health benefits of gratitude.* https://www.uclahealth.org/news/article/health-benefits-gratitude

Victor Staff (2023). From anxiety to advocacy: A Victor success story. *Victor.* https://blog.victor.org/from-anxiety-to-advocacy

Wehrenberg, M. (2005). *Ten best-ever anxiety-management techniques.* Psychotherapy Networker. https://www.psychotherapynetworker.org/article/ten-best-ever-anxiety-management-techniques/

*What Is Exposure Therapy?* (2017). American Psychological Association. https://www.apa.org/ptsd-guideline/patients-and-families/exposure-therapy

Wilmer, M. T., Anderson, K., & Reynolds, M. (2021). Correlates of Quality of Life in Anxiety Disorders:

Review of Recent Research. *Current Psychiatry Reports*, *23*(11). https://doi.org/10.1007/s11920-021-01290-4

Wu, T., Luo, Y., Broster, L. S., Gu, R., & Luo, Y. (2012, June 6). The impact of anxiety on social decision-making: Behavioral and electrodermal findings. *Social Neuroscience*, *8*(1), 11. https://doi.org/10.1080/17470919.2012.694372

Yeager, D. S., & Dweck, C. S. (2020). What can be learned from growth mindset controversies? *The American Psychologist*, *75*(9), 1269. https://doi.org/10.1037/amp0000794

Zaider, T. I., Heimberg, R. G., & Iida, M. (2010). Anxiety disorders and intimate relationships: a study of daily processes in couples. *Journal of Abnormal Psychology*, *119*(1), 163. https://doi.org/10.1037/a0018473

Zgierska, A., & Burzinski, C.. (2014). *Reducing relapse risk*. VA.gov. https://www.va.gov/WHOLEHEALTHLIBRARY/tools/reducing-relapse-risk.asp

Zhao, Y., & Paulus, M. et al. (2023). Study Probes Connection Between Excessive Screen Media Activity and Mental Health Problems in Youth. *Journal of Behavioral Addictions*. https://doi.org/10.10.1234/jba.2023.4567